KATARINA JOHNSON-THOMPSON

ULTIMATE SPORTS HEROES

KATARINA JOHNSON-THOMPSON

GOING FOR GOLD

DINO

First published by Dino Books in 2021,
an imprint of Bonnier Books UK,
The Plaza, 535 King's Road, London SW10 0SZ
Owned by Bonnier Books,
Sveavägen 56, Stockholm, Sweden

🔲 @dinobooks
www.bonnierbooks.co.uk

© Dino Books
Written by Melanie Hamm
Cover illustration by Bruce Huang

Paperback ISBN: 9781789463019
Ebook ISBN: 9781789464375

British Library cataloguing-in-publication data:
A catalogue record for this book is available from the British Library.

Printed and bound in Great Britain by Clays Lltd, Elcograf S.p.A.

1 3 5 7 9 10 8 6 4 2

For Nina

TABLE OF CONTENTS

PROLOGUE

It was a sunny April day on Australia's Gold Coast. Here, down under, it was autumn, but on the track at the Carrara Stadium, the athletes were wiping the sweat from their brows. It was as hot as a British summer's day.

Katarina Johnson-Thompson looked around the stadium, squinting to shield her eyes from the blazing sun. The stands were packed, including a generous number of bright yellow tops: Australian supporters wearing their national colour. Her fellow heptathletes came from eight Commonwealth nations, among them Canada, India, Belize, Ghana

– and of course, Australia. And because it was the Commonwealth Games, Kat, competing for England, would be running, jumping and throwing against athletes from Scotland and Northern Ireland.

Kat turned her focus back to the track and the long row of hurdles stretching out in front of her. The 100-metres hurdles was the first event of the seven that made up the heptathlon. Nerves fluttered in Kat's stomach. The hurdles were never her favourite event. The pressure always felt greatest at the start of the competition, and today she felt it more strongly than ever.

Although Kat was the reigning world indoor champion, she had never won an international competition outdoors – not since junior level. Over the last few years, she had experienced setback after setback, including battles with injury and self-confidence. Here on the Gold Coast, she had everything to prove.

But as she stood on the track in the bright

Australian sunshine, Kat felt a glow of positivity. Determination sparkled in her eyes. It was time to turn things around. She was ready!

The arena fell silent as Kat and her fellow athletes stepped into their blocks. But as the starting gun fired, the crowd erupted into noisy cheers of support. Kat made a strong start, springing nimbly over the first hurdles. But she had competition. On one side of her, Angela Whyte from Canada stormed into first place; on the other, Australian Celeste Mucci and the Canadian Nina Schultz moved into second and third.

Kat urged herself forward. She was pulling level with Nina in third. *Faster! Come on!*

But pressure from Kat sent the Canadian powering over the final few hurdles. Kat couldn't catch her. To the delight of the home crowd, Celeste, the Australian, finished first.

With six more events to go, Kat had plenty more opportunities to pick up points! Next was the high jump, her strongest discipline.

The English fans whooped as Kat flew elegantly over the crossbar, landing a stunning jump of 1.87 metres, taking her into first place.

The shot put was next. By now, night had fallen over the stadium, and blazing floodlights added to the sense of drama. Kat's heart was pounding as she stood in the throwing circle. This event was her weak point.

Kat frowned: 11.54 metres. It was over two metres short of the winning throw. From first position, Kat had slipped into third.

But the evening wasn't over. The final event of the day, the 200 metres, was one of Kat's strongest. It was time to deliver a rocket-propelled sprint!

And that's exactly what Kat did. Accompanied by enthusiastic whoops and cheers from the crowd, Kat powered straight into the lead. The other racers pounded the track, straining to catch her, but Kat was flying. *Over the line! Back in first place!*

Kat felt a glow of satisfaction as the day ended.

She knew to take nothing for granted in the heptathlon – with three events still to go, anything could happen. But for now, as the stars glittered high above the Carrara Stadium, Kat was in the lead. Gold-medal position!

Day two of the heptathlon dawned grey and overcast, but the enthusiasm of the crowd was as warm and noisy as ever. Kat felt a surge of excitement as she launched into her fifth event, the long jump. This was another of her best disciplines. She allowed herself a flicker of a smile as she clocked her distance: 6.50 metres. A strong jump. She had increased her overall lead.

And she was *still* in the lead after the javelin round.

As the runners lined up for the final event, the 800 metres, she gave a broad grin for the TV cameras. It was time to relax and enjoy herself!

As the starting gun fired, Angela Whyte strode into first place. Niamh Emerson, Kat's England teammate, darted into a strong second, followed by

Nina Schultz in third.

Kat trailed them in fourth. With two laps of the track to run, there was plenty of time to push forward. But when the moment came to make her move, her legs wouldn't let her. There was sharp pain in her right calf that grew with every stride.

Keep up, Kat told herself. *Keep up. That's enough.*

A painful two minutes later, Kat stumbled across the line in fourth. Her teammate, Niamh, had crossed the line in first. But a glance at the leaderboard sent Kat's heart soaring. She hadn't won the race, but victory was still hers! With a score more than 100 points higher than her closest rival, Nina Schultz, she, Katarina Johnson-Thompson, was the Commonwealth gold medallist!

As the gold medal was looped around her neck, Kat's pain was forgotten. Pride and jubilation flowed through her. This was her moment. Her first international gold!

And as the National Anthem played, Kat's mind flew ahead to the future. Following the

Commonwealth Games were the European Championships, then the World Championships, then the Tokyo Olympics. Standing here on the podium, it felt like the whole world was at her feet.

And Kat was determined to make a habit of winning!

CHAPTER 1

NASSAU

It was Tracey Johnson's first visit to the beautiful Caribbean island of New Providence in the Bahamas. She had come here as a dancer. Her troupe, the famous Bluebell Girls, performed all over the world: Paris, Rome, Madrid, New York, Toronto – and now Nassau, capital of the Bahamas. Every destination was special to the young dancers, and for Tracey, the trip to Nassau was to prove more special than most.

It was on Nassau's glittering beachfront, at the lavish Crystal Palace Hotel, that Tracey met her future husband, Ricardo Thompson. Tracey was performing there. Ricky was working at the hotel as a bellboy. There could be no more romantic setting to fall in love in, and that's exactly what Tracey did... with Ricky, and with this stunning Caribbean island.

Five years later, Tracey was still here in Nassau. She and Ricky had been together ever since that first magical meeting – and they were now expecting their first child. The couple decided to travel back to the UK for the birth. They reluctantly swapped the warm beaches and rustling palms of Nassau for the grey winter skies of Liverpool, home to Tracey's family. How cold it seemed to Ricky. How wet. How loud and bustling. Tracey too had got used to the sunshine of Nassau, the relaxed holiday vibe. Merseyside was going to take some getting used to!

On 9 January 1993, in the Liverpool suburb of Woolton, Katarina Mary Johnson-Thompson was born. Outside the rain was still falling, the sky was still grey. But as they bent over their newborn daughter, it was as if the Caribbean sun shone down on Tracey and Ricky. Around them, nurses and doctors smiled at the couple's delight.

'She's perfect!' said Ricky, rocking his tiny daughter in his arms.

'Little Katarina,' breathed Tracey. 'I wonder who she'll grow up to be.'

As the weeks and months went by, Ricky and Tracey watched as their little girl grew and grew. Every day brought new excitements. Smiles, gurgles, first words... Tracey and Ricky were enchanted, and they couldn't wait to take baby Katarina back to their island paradise.

First, though, they decided to get married. Friends and family gathered at the local registry office to listen as they exchanged their vows. Among the smiling faces was Katarina's, snuggled in the arms of her grandmother. Her happy squeals punctuated the ceremony.

'Do you have to go back to the Bahamas so soon?' asked her grandma.

'We miss it,' said Tracey. 'And we want little Kat to see it.'

It was true. Ricky and Tracey longed for their beautiful Caribbean home. Their plane tickets were booked, their bags packed, and one smiling baby was the final piece of very important luggage.

So, just a few months after Katarina's birth, the family was back in their small home in Nassau. Now it was the turn of Ricky's family and neighbours to meet little Kat. Wriggling and giggling in her pushchair, blinking her big brown eyes, Kat was adored by everyone. Even strangers on the street couldn't help grinning when they saw her.

'She's a blessing.'

'A very special baby.'

'A lucky baby.'

And of course, her parents agreed. Their beloved Kat was all of these things!

Tracey and Ricky soon settled into a happy routine. Ricky went back to his job at the Crystal Palace Hotel and rushed home after his shift to play with his little daughter, who was growing cleverer and more active every day.

But their bubble of contentment was about to be broken...

A year after returning from Liverpool to Nassau, Ricky came home from work with bad news.

'They're closing the hotel. Shutting it down completely. Tracey, I'm going to lose my job.'

Tracey stared at him in disbelief. 'They're shutting down the Crystal Palace? But – they can't! It's – it's—'

Tracey was lost for words. The huge Crystal Palace Hotel was the biggest landmark on the island. Its glittering towers, lit in rainbow colours at night, were the first thing visitors saw when they arrived by boat or plane. And of course, it was particularly special to her and Ricky. Without it, they would never have met.

Ricky hugged her. 'I'll look for work. It'll be okay.'

But as the weeks went on, it became clear that jobs were scarce. The hotel employed hundreds of staff members. It had been one of the biggest employers on the island. Some of the workers – waiters, porters, chefs, cleaners, receptionists – found jobs elsewhere, but many didn't, including Ricky.

'I wish I could help,' Tracey told him. But as a foreigner, it was almost impossible for her to find work.

Eventually the couple came to a painful decision. Tracey and baby Katarina would move back to the UK, where Tracey could find a job and support their daughter. Ricky would visit, and Tracey and Katarina would come back to the Bahamas whenever they could.

Ricky was heartbroken. 'But it's the only way to give her a future,' he said, cuddling Katarina tightly. 'The only way.'

So, with a heavy heart, Tracey packed her suitcases once again. This time it was for good.

CHAPTER 2

TOMBOY IN A TUTU

Tracey and her daughter settled in Woolton, the Liverpool suburb where Katarina had been born, moving into the house shared by Tracey's mother, father and aunt. How different it was from Nassau, with its brightly coloured houses, sandy beach cafés and luminous turquoise sea. Swaying palms were replaced by ancient oaks and beech trees, and the bright sunshine by the changeable British weather: sun, showers, wind, hail...

From Woolton, with its big, comfortable houses, and its leafy parks and shops, it was a short bus ride to the centre of Liverpool. Here Tracey strolled around the iconic Albert Dock, with baby Kat in her pushchair. Everywhere she went there were reminders of the two things for which Liverpool was most famous: the Beatles, and Liverpool Football Club, or 'the Reds', who played at the city stadium, Anfield.

Tracey found work. She enrolled the lively Kat in nursery, and found a local ballet class for her as soon as she could toddle. Tracey missed her life as a dancer – the glitz and glamour, the thrill of being onstage... But she hoped Katarina might fall in love with ballet too. Tracey was determined to give her daughter the opportunity to follow in her footsteps, to discover this wonderful world of dance for herself.

Little Katarina was keen to please her mum. She went off to ballet class with a smile on her face, clutching a dance bag with her pink ballet shoes inside. She let Tracey dress her in a tutu and brush her dark curly hair into a neat little bun. Her mum came to watch the class sometimes, and Kat made sure to remember all the steps and smile while she did them. She knew how much her mum loved to watch her.

As the years went on, there were shows and ballet exams too. The walls of Kat's bedroom filled up with certificates, while her wardrobe filled up with leotards, tights and tutus. Her weekly schedule filled up with classes – ballet and tap. Kat was strong and graceful. All her teachers encouraged her, and Tracey started to get excited: her daughter had the makings of a professional dancer. Tracey's dream? That Kat would get a place at the Royal Ballet School. How proud she would be!

But Kat had a secret. She didn't really enjoy this world of pink and satin and spinning around to tinkling piano music. She would much rather be outside playing football! Her grandfather had introduced her to Anfield and Liverpool FC at a young age. Wearing her Liverpool shirt – Steven Gerrard, Number 8 – Katarina played as often as she could in the street near her house.

At school, St Mark's Primary in Woolton, sport

was quickly becoming Kat's favourite subject. She was one of the fastest runners in her class. Her teachers praised her sportsmanship and her determination. Kat was shy and quiet, but she had a strong competitive spirit.

'I'm going to win gold in the 100 metres this year,' she told her mum when the end-of-year Sports Day came round. 'Will you come and watch?'

'Of course.' Tracey hugged her. 'I wouldn't miss it for the world.'

Sports Day was Kat's favourite day of the whole year. She could hardly contain her excitement. As she sat impatiently through morning English and Maths lessons, her thoughts weren't on spellings or fractions. Her mind was already out on the field. She imagined the wind in her hair as she ran faster, faster, faster...

After lunch, it was finally time for the whole school to gather outside on the playing field. As usual, the teachers had organised all sorts of competitions: running, long jumping, relays – and even a sack race. Kat beat her classmates in almost everything. Crossing the finish line in first position and hearing Tracey's cheers of delight gave her a warm glow of pride!

Eventually it was time for the 100-metres final, the last race of the day. Only the fastest children were competing. As they waited on the start line, Kat felt a thrill of nerves and excitement. She grinned at Tracey who gave her an enthusiastic thumbs-up.

The Head of PE, Mr Willis, shouted, 'Ready, set, *go!*'

Kat and her schoolmates bounded away across the grass. The families shouted their encouragement. Kat reached maximum speed in just a few strides. Her feet were pounding the ground. Her arms were pumping. She couldn't go any faster. But wait – someone was catching her up. *No!* Kat eyed the finish line. Suddenly she found she could go faster. Her stride grew longer. Her arms pumped faster. She heard Tracey cheering. Without even noticing, she had crossed the line.

'Well done, Katarina! That was a brilliant run!' declared Mr Willis. He waited a moment while the runners got their breath back. 'Now, let's give out those medals!'

The kids who had come second and third stepped onto the podium. Shy Kat felt a flutter of nerves. Winning meant she would have to stand up there in front of everyone!

'And the gold medal goes to Katarina Johnson-Thompson!'

Eek! Here goes! Katarina stepped onto the podium and Mr Willis looped a shiny gold-coloured medal around her neck. There was loud applause from her schoolmates and their families. Kat beamed as Tracey took her picture. She loved the feeling of a medal hanging heavy around her neck!

And she couldn't wait for the chance to run again. She wanted to find out if she could push her legs even faster.

* * *

Kat was nine when she finally plucked up the courage to tell Tracey how she felt about ballet. She was quivering inside as she searched for the right words to use. She hated the idea of upsetting her mother.

'Mum, I–I–I don't think I want to do ballet anymore. I'm not enjoying it.' She paused, waiting for Tracey's reaction. 'Mum?'

Her mum stared back at her and Kat was worried she might cry.

At last Tracey spoke. 'But you've worked so hard, Kat. You've got so much promise as a dancer. Do you really want to give it all up?'

Kat nodded silently. She watched a tear rolled down her mum's cheek, and a guilty feeling clawed at her stomach.

But then her mum spoke again. 'It's okay, my love. I understand.' Tracey hugged her.

Kat felt like a heavy weight had lifted from her

shoulders. 'So does this mean I don't have to go to ballet class any more?'

'You don't have to do anything you don't want to do. I only wish you'd told me sooner, Kat.'

Kat beamed at her. 'You're not angry?' she asked.

'How could I be angry with you?' Tracey replied. 'You've tried your best. You've given your all.' Her daughter *always* gave her all. 'I'm so proud of everything you've achieved. I just want you to be happy, my love.'

So it was settled. No more ballet. No more leotards and tutus. No more dance exams. Her mum had just one condition: Kat needed another hobby to replace dancing.

Football?

Learning the keyboard?

Drama classes?

There were lots of options, and Kat tried them all. But nothing seemed to stick. It was running – running really, *really* fast – that made Kat happiest.

But running wasn't a hobby – was it?

CHAPTER 3

TAKING A LEAP

'But I've never tried the high jump,' gulped ten-year-old Katarina. 'What if I can't do it?'

Mr Coakley, her teacher, smiled. 'You'll never find out if you don't give it a go, Kat. Here, we'll set the bar low to start with.'

The bar was a bamboo pole, taped to two metal stands. Below was a crash mat. A group of pupils, all wearing yellow St Mark's PE kits, had gathered around to watch.

Kat bent her knees and got ready to leap.

'You get a run-up,' said Mr Coakley, smiling.

Ah! Kat backed away from the pole to the other

side of the gym hall. She started to sprint towards the mat and the spindly bamboo pole, her long legs taking her higher with each step.

'Now, jump,' said her teacher.

Kat leapt into the air. She had expected to hear the crack of splintering bamboo as she crashed into the pole – but no! She sailed easily over it.

'Very good!' cried Mr Coakley. 'A round of applause for Kat's first high jump, please.'

Kat's classmates burst into loud applause. 'Go, Kat! Go, Kat!'

Kat beamed from ear to ear. 'Can I try a bit higher?'

Mr Coakley grinned. He'd known Kat's competitive spirit would quickly kick in. He raised the pole by a few centimetres. Once again, Kat bounded across the hall and cleared the pole with plenty of room to spare.

'Still too easy for you, eh, Kat?' he said. 'Let's give you a real challenge.' He raised the pole again. 'You can do it.'

Kat frowned. The pole looked really high this time. Surely she couldn't leap over that?

She shook out her legs. This time her run-up was slower, more calculated. She kept the pole in her sight with every step, and just as it seemed she was about to hit it, she leapt into the air, throwing every bit of energy into sending herself skyward.

She landed with a thump on the crash mat as her classmates let out a cheer.

'I did it?'

Mr Coakley's face was a mix of surprise and delight. 'You did it. You actually did it!'

Kat spun round. Yes, the pole had remained exactly where it was! She hadn't so much as touched it.

'Someone fetch a tape measure from the office,' Mr Coakley requested. 'Quickly. I think we might have a record here.'

Kat looked confused. A record?

Mr Coakley explained. 'The school high jump record has been in place for 29 years. It was set long before my time. But I have a feeling...'

A pupil came running back with the tape measure. Under the teacher's instruction, Kat and her classmates took the measurement.

'Just as I thought. Katarina Johnson-Thompson, you are officially a record holder! Twenty-nine years. My, my, this is quite an achievement.'

A grin lit up Katarina's face. She could hardly believe it. Until today she had never even tried the high jump! She couldn't wait to tell Tracey.

Mr Coakley looked thoughtful. 'I think you could have something special here, Kat. Now, off you go, kids, it's breaktime. Quietly now. I said – quietly!'

The children hurried out to the playground, sweeping Katarina up in an excited hubbub.

Mr Coakley shook his head in disbelief. 'That was extraordinary,' he said to himself. 'I can barely believe it. Imagine what she'd be able to do with some training.'

And an idea popped into his head.

The Harriers.

Later that afternoon, while Katarina recounted her record-breaking jump to Tracey back at home, Mr Coakley made a call to the Liverpool Harriers. Everyone in the city knew about the Harriers. They were one of the most famous athletics clubs in the country, founded 150 years ago. The Harriers team competed all over the country in all sorts of events: running, jumping, throwing, hurdles, cross country, marathon – the list went on and on. Their coaches were among the best in the UK and they were always on the lookout for talented young athletes to join their junior section.

Katarina was ten, old enough to join the junior section, and the Harriers arranged for a scout to come and watch her perform. Kat could barely contain her excitement. She felt a thrill that she had never felt before a ballet show. The Harriers! Training from professional coaches! She had never wanted anything so badly.

When the day came to perform for the scout,

Kat excelled. She pushed herself to run even faster than usual. She impressed the scout with her high jump and her long jump – and with her calm determination. Her strength of focus was clear to everyone watching.

'She's got potential,' the scout declared. Turning to Kat, he asked, 'Would you like to join the Harriers, Katarina?'

Kat could only nod. Her head was spinning. She knew she had done her best, but she had hardly dared hope they might want her.

Her teacher spoke for her. 'I think that's a yes!' he said.

At last, Kat found her voice. 'Yes! Yes, thank you!' she gasped. 'Oh, I'll train so hard. I won't let you down! Thank you!'

CHAPTER 4

THE HARRIERS

Athletics was just the hobby that Kat had been looking for. The Harriers junior section trained on Tuesday night and Kat fizzed with excitement every time she waited for the bus to take her from school to the grounds. In her bag was her yellow Harriers vest with its blue harrier logo, her most treasured possession.

Kat's coach was Val Rutter. Along with the Harriers' head coach, Mike Holmes, Val trained some of the Harriers' best athletes – some of them had gone on to perform on the UK athletics team. Young Katarina was a natural athlete, everyone could see that. Expectations were high – and training this talented newcomer would be a serious matter!

Kat's running was already strong. Under Val's instruction, she learnt the difference between sprinting and longer races. Val showed her how to spring out of the blocks and deliver a rocket-paced sprint. She taught Kat how to run longer races, conserving her energy so she didn't run out of puff halfway around the track. She was delighted to find out that Kat was good at both!

Next Val introduced Kat to hurdles. For several weeks, they did practice drills, learning techniques. Val showed her how to swing her legs over the hurdle one at time. Then Kat practised jumping over, leading with one leg then the other.

'My legs ache,' Kat grimaced. 'In weird places!'

Val smiled. 'Then you're doing something right. Hurdling uses a whole new set of muscles. I think you're ready to try the real thing now, Kat.'

Outside on the running track, Val had set up a line of hurdles, waist-high barriers planted at intervals of several metres all the way along the lane.

'This is a tough event,' she explained. 'Hurdles require speed, strength and flexibility, as well as coordination and balance. Think you can do it?'

Kat was always up for a challenge. Her legs were tingling and her mind was already whirring, calculating how to combine the sprint, the jump and the landing.

'I'll give it a go!' she grinned.

'The most important thing is not to hesitate in front of the hurdle. That's how people get hurt. Just go for it, Kat!'

Kat bounded fearlessly off the starting line towards the first hurdle. Safely over! The next hurdle loomed immediately. Over again! It was only when she got to the last hurdle that she stumbled. Her foot caught the top and she toppled to the ground. She rolled on to her back with a laugh.

'That was great for a first attempt, Kat,' said Val. 'Let's try again. And don't leap too high. That'll take away your momentum.'

This time Kat cleared all the hurdles cleanly. 'Is there anything you're not good at, Katarina?' laughed Val.

Kat scrunched up her face. 'Er... throwing?' Throwing had always been her weak point. At school there were lots of kids who were much better than she was.

'We'll work on it,' Val told her.

So they did. The next session began in the throwing circle. Kat and her junior teammates were going to learn the shot put.

First they passed the 'shot' around the group so everyone could feel the weight of it.

'It's so heavy! What if it lands on our feet?' one girl asked.

'Has anyone ever got hit?'

'Can we spin around before throwing it, like they do on TV?' said another.

Val looked stern. 'No hitting each other, please. And no spinning. That's called a "wind-up" and it's much, much harder.' She took the shot and raised it to her jaw. 'Right, step back and watch, everyone.'

With Kat and her friends at a safe distance, Val balanced herself at the edge of the circle. She made a sharp half-turn, and flung her arm out, sending the shot soaring through the air before it thudded down onto the grass.

'How did you make it go so far?' Kat asked in amazement.

Val explained. 'The trick is to use your whole body for momentum, not just your throwing arm.' She demonstrated again. 'See – my legs are bent and when I turn, my whole body is powering the shot. Let's do some drills. We'll start off without the shot.'

The group groaned. They hated drills. They wanted to start throwing straight away. But not Katarina. She loved to learn new techniques. For every event there were tricks to learn to make her performance the best it could possibly be. She listened attentively as Val told them how to hold the shot, how to stand, and the best way to shift their weight from one leg to the other.

But when they started to throw, Kat didn't find it easy. She visualised the shot flying long over the grass. In reality, it travelled just a few metres before falling back to the earth. Everyone else's shots were going further.

It was the same when they tried the javelin. Kat's legs gave her momentum, but her shoulders and arms weren't strong enough to give power to the throw. The frustration showed in her face.

'Early days, Kat,' Val told her.

But in the long jump and high jump, Kat shone. Mr Coakley's bamboo pole was a distant memory. Now Kat and her friends trained with a proper high jump: a pole supported by a stand, and a landing area as thick and bouncy as a trampoline. Kat was tall for her age, and her long legs helped her spring up and over the crossbar, landing impressive jumps. In the long jump, she bounded energetically along the run-up, sprang gracefully from the take-off board and kicked her legs in mid-air before landing in the sandpit. Each time she jumped further and her smile got broader. This was so much fun!

As the months went by, Val became more and more impressed with her protégée. Not only was Katarina talented, but of all the young athletes she trained, Kat was also the most dedicated. Even on the darkest, coldest winter evenings, when the other kids would start to drop away, preferring warm living rooms and the glow of their phone and TV screens, Kat would always be out there on the track, training under the floodlights with a smile on her face. She was determined to push herself as hard as she possibly could – and Val was determined to give her all the support she needed.

So too was Tracey. Kat's decision to swap tights and tutus for track and field had disappointed her mum – but she knew deep down that it was the right choice. She celebrated her daughter's achievements session by session with just as much enthusiasm as she had celebrated her ballet successes. Meanwhile, in the Bahamas, Ricky also followed Kat's progress, his face glowing with pride and pleasure as she told him all about her training on the phone.

Kat had found her passion, and supporting her from both sides of the globe, her parents could not be happier.

CHAPTER 5

TRACK TRIUMPH

In January 2005, Kat turned 12. She had moved from her small primary school, St Mark's, to nearby St Julie's Catholic High School, where she made a group of firm friends: Jodie, Olivia, Charlotte and Lauren. The girls all had their passions. Jodie, for instance, loved English and acting. She was in every one of their school plays and performances and wanted to be an actress.

Kat worked hard in all subjects, but sport remained her favourite. She was shy and modest, but all her friends knew her dream: to be a professional sportsperson.

The Harriers' sports ground in Wavertree, south Liverpool, had rapidly become Kat's second home. Her skills and strength were improving every week, and Val eventually knew she was ready to start competing.

The Harriers Under-13 Girls were part of the Youth Athletics Northern Premier League. Kat would be competing at the most iconic arenas in the north of England: the Gateshead International Stadium, the Don Valley in Sheffield... This was the moment Kat had been waiting for!

Her first year of competition brought a flurry of successes:

The Merseyside County Championships in Liverpool: first in the high jump.

Blackpool Open Medal Meeting: first in the 800 metres.

The Youth Athletics League Final in Birmingham: first in the 70-metres hurdles; third in the high jump.

Kat's bedroom was quickly filling up with medals.

But it wasn't just about winning. Kat was part

of a team now. She loved cheering on the other Harriers girls almost as much as she loved being out on the track herself. All the points that the girls won contributed to a team total, and the Under-13s were storming up the League. Indoors, outdoors, rain or shine, nothing could keep the smile from Kat's face.

But the world of competition brought new challenges. In athletics, anything could go wrong at any moment. A stumble in the hurdles. A sudden gust of wind. The flick of a ponytail knocking a wobbling crossbar off its stand. The road to success wasn't always smooth and Kat's confidence was easily dented by a mistake or a disappointing performance. She hated the feeling that she could have done better. And the more success she had, the more she struggled with self-doubt when she failed to come first.

But a sense of confidence and resilience came to Kat from a surprising source.

After athletics, Kat's biggest passion was for

Liverpool FC. Over the years, she had seen them rise to glory than fall dramatically back down the league table. It was a rollercoaster of emotions for their fans – including 12-year-old Kat.

On 25 May 2005, Kat was glued to the TV as Liverpool played in the UEFA Champions League Final against AC Milan at the Atatürk Olympic Stadium in Istanbul, Turkey. Milan were the favourites. If Liverpool didn't win, they would not qualify for the competition next year. All Kat's hopes were on the pitch with her beloved Reds.

There was instant disappointment. Within the first minute, Milan's captain, Paolo Maldini, scored. Kat howled with despair. Too soon!

Twelve nail-biting minutes later, Milan scored again. As the Milan fans cheered, the camera panned to the Liverpool crowd, their faces wide-eyed with dismay. Kat could hardly watch. Her team defended attack after attack. Surely they couldn't hold out much longer?

They didn't. Another Milan goal followed. The

first half ended 3–0.

That's that, Kat thought. *It's over.* Along with hundreds of millions of fans across the country, she was resigned to Liverpool losing.

But as the second half began, Liverpool's fortunes seemed to be turning. They missed two chances. Then Steven Gerrard scored with a header. 3–1! Kat's heart thudded in her chest – from dark despair, there was a glimmer of hope. The cheers of the Liverpool crowd were ear-splitting.

Minutes later there was another Liverpool goal, from Vladimir Šmicer. 3–2!

Then another, from Xabi Alonso. 3–3!

Was it possible? Could Liverpool actually win the match?

But Kat's joy was mixed with anxiety. There were still twenty minutes to go! She watched, barely able to breathe, as the ball flew from one side of the pitch to the other. Liverpool attacked. Milan defended. Milan attacked. Liverpool defended. At the final whistle the score remained 3–3.

The match would go to extra time.

Kat could see how tired the players were – but every one of them continued to give their all. Both Liverpool and Milan had chances, defended desperately by their goalies. The crowd were on their feet. The tension was extraordinary.

When the referee's whistle blew again, it was to signal a penalty shoot-out.

As the TV commentator reeled out penalty statistics, Kat's eyes were fixed on the Liverpool strikers, led by Steven Gerrard, the captain. Could they keep their focus? Would the Milan goalie make a mistake? Worse, would the Liverpool goalie make a mistake?

Milan took the first penalty. The ball hit the crossbar – and Kat squealed with delight.

Dietmar Hamann stepped up to take the next shot for Liverpool. The ball flew into the net! Kat cheered. 1–0!

Milan's next shot was heading straight for the back of the net – but the goalie dived low to save it.

Still 1–0.

Liverpool scored next. 2–0!

Milan scored. 2–1.

Liverpool's next penalty was saved by the Milan goalie. Oh no – was the tide turning again?

Milan scored with the next kick. 2–2.

Vladimír Šmicer was next to kick for Liverpool. The ball flew into the back of the net. Liverpool were 3–2 up.

Milan's Andriy Shevchenko stepped up. Kat gripped the edge of the sofa. If he missed, Liverpool would win. She stared at the TV, unblinking, watching as the ball shot towards the back of the net. The goalkeeper, Jerzy Dudek, hurled himself to the right – the wrong way! But suddenly Dudek's arm shot out to the left, stopping the ball. The penalty was saved. Liverpool had won!

Finally, Kat drew breath. Along with ten thousand fans in the stadium, and hundreds of millions worldwide, she let out an ecstatic cheer of joy and relief. No one had expected this. The Reds had won against all the odds. Even the manager, Rafael Benítez, looked shocked.

The match in Istanbul would stick in Kat's mind for ever. The memory would return to her whenever she felt herself falling behind, whenever her confidence was low. She had learned a valuable lesson.

Anything was possible. Never rule out the underdog!

CHAPTER 6

INDECISION

Under Val's dedicated coaching, Kat continued to shine in the high jump and long jump. Her skills in the other events were going from strength to strength too. She was training five days a week now, and her strength, stamina and skill were constantly improving.

But as Kat's collection of trophies and medals continued to grow, her friends and family had a question on their minds.

'Which event do you like best?' asked her friend Jodie. 'Do you know what you want to specialise in?'

Specialise? Kat frowned. She knew that most

athletes ended up focusing on one event. But it hadn't occurred to her that she too would have to choose between the sports she loved. She liked jumping, of course. High jump and long jump were where she got her biggest scores. But she also loved to challenge herself. Throwing? She was getting better at throwing at every session. She enjoyed the feeling of working hard and seeing the results each week.

'I–I don't know,' she stammered. 'I love all of them. I couldn't decide.'

Jodie grinned. 'Typical Kat! So indecisive!'

It was true. Kat was known for her indecision. Whether it was pizza toppings or what to wear to go out, Katarina always struggled to choose. Her friend didn't have that problem. Whereas Kat threw her energy into everything she did, Jodie was focused on drama, and drama alone – to the frustration of her other teachers!

'Maybe I won't have to decide.' Kat's face lit up. 'There's always the heptathlon. I could be a heptathlete.'

'Like Denise Lewis?'

'Exactly.'

Katarina loved to watch the heptathletes competing. She admired how versatile and skilled they were, like athletic superheroes! Of course, she enjoyed the drama and excitement of the big sprint races, the 100 and 200 metres. The sprinters were the megastars of the arena. But she followed the fortunes of the 'multi-eventers' with particular interest. The heptathlon, for the women, was all about endurance: seven events across two days. They started with the 100-metres hurdles, followed by the high jump, then the shot put and the 200 metres on day one. Day two was the long jump, the javelin, and finally the 800 metres. Meanwhile, the men competed in a 10-event version called the decathlon. In both cases, the points system was complicated. Kat watched with fascination as the athletes' scores accumulated between events. She got to know who was strongest in which discipline and where their weaknesses lay. She liked hard work – and no one in athletics worked harder than the heptathletes!

It turned out Val was thinking about the heptathlon too.

'It makes sense,' Val told Mike Holmes. 'Her high jump is outstanding, but she's so versatile too. She really is good at everything.'

Head coach Mike had been taking a keen interest in Kat's progress since she joined the team. He nodded. 'Let's train her for the heptathlon. I can't wait to see what she can do.'

So it was settled. It was time to combine Kat's skills. She would be a heptathlete and she couldn't wait!

In August 2006, 13-year-old Kat took part in her first multi-event competition: the pentathlon at the Amateur Athletic Association Under-15s Combined Events Championships. Pentathlons featured just five out of the seven events of the heptathlon: no javelin or 100 metres. At indoor events, the pentathlon always replaced the heptathlon – for a start, there simply wasn't room to throw a javelin indoors!

Kat finished sixth at the end of the competition, scoring a total of 2,748 points.

'Good job, Kat,' said Val with a smile.

From the sidelines, her mum had watched every step, jump and throw. 'I'm so proud of you, darling!' she said. 'That was amazing.'

Kat had earned her highest ever scores in long jump and high jump, competing against older girls. Running, jumping and throwing against the older teenagers hadn't phased her. She had loved the buzz of the stadium and the thrill of a tough competition.

'I had so much fun,' she beamed. 'I can't wait to try the full heptathlon!'

Kat's performance had given her an Under-15s pentathlon ranking of 15th in the country. She was ranked number 34 for the long jump and tenth for the high jump. Val and Mike knew this was just the start, though. Talented Kat had much, much more to give, they were sure of it.

They were right. The following year, 2007, Kat won gold at the Sainsbury's English Schools Championships; gold in the high jump at the England Athletics Under-15s Open Championships; gold in the high jump at the English Schools Combined Events pentathlon; gold in the England Athletics Under-15s Open Combined Events Championships pentathlon; gold at the England Athletics Under-15s Open Combined Events Indoor Championships pentathlon.

'This is getting silly,' laughed Jodie. 'No one needs that many medals! What ranking are you now, Kat?'

Kat shrugged modestly. 'Well, um, second in the Under-15s long jump. First in the high jump. And first in the pentathlon.'

'Seriously!' Jodie let out a squeal. 'Kat, that's incredible. Why do you keep this stuff to yourself? It's amazing!'

Kat blushed. 'They're just numbers, aren't they?'

'Just numbers?' squealed Jodie. 'Just numbers! You're one of the best young athletes in the country. In. The. Country.'

'Jodie Comer!' Kat ruffled her friend's hair. 'What about you? You danced for Craig Revel Horwood!'

It was true. Jodie and a group of girls from their school had won a national competition, Boogie For Your Bones, judged by the most brutal of the *Strictly Come Dancing* judges, Craig.

'But you don't see me making a secret of it, do you!' laughed Jodie. 'Unlike you, national champ!'

It was becoming harder to for Kat to keep her athletics success quiet though. In 2008, she won another string of gold medals, at the Under-17s Indoor Championships, the English Schools Championships, English Schools Combined Events and the England Athletics Open Championships. And while *she* didn't like to shout about her achievements, her teachers did. Shy, modest Kat hated assemblies where her name was read out and the whole school turned to stare at her. Being in the spotlight made her want to shrink into the floor – especially with Jodie and her other friends whooping noisily by her side!

CHAPTER 7

ITALIAN JOB

Warm Mediterranean sunshine was streaming down on a packed sports stadium in the small town of Bressanone, in northern Italy. Kat had never seen such a beautiful location for an arena. The track was fringed by lush fir trees. Beyond the trees were rolling green hills, with huge cloud-topped mountains in the distance. The sky was a luminous blue and the air was crystal pure. Kat breathed deeply and took in the scene with shining eyes.

The stands were packed with spectators, enjoying the sunshine and eagerly awaiting the first events. There were journalists too – for this was the World

Youth Championships, Kat's first international competition. All her competitions so far, all of her training and hard work had been leading to this moment, when she would compete alongside athletes from Europe, Africa, Asia, the USA, and even her dad's home country, the Bahamas.

The pressure was on. It was 2009 and the London Olympics, in 2012, were already on everyone's lips. Among these teenage sportspeople were future Olympians. Would 16-year-old Kat be one of them? To compete at the London Olympics was her goal, her dream...

First though, she needed to impress here in Italy.

So far, Kat's best combined score was 5,343. Her points tally had been rocketing upwards with every competition, but she knew she could still do better. Her secret hope? To achieve personal bests in all seven disciplines.

Day one began, as usual, with the 100-metres hurdles. Kat always felt nervous about the hurdles. There was so much that could go wrong. If she tripped over just one hurdle, the race would be over.

But she needn't have worried. As soon as the starting gun fired, she was away, sailing effortlessly over the hurdles. As she charged over the line, the cheers of the crowd rang in her ears. A personal best! What a way to start the competition!

Now that the hurdles were over, Kat felt more relaxed. She was enjoying herself in the bright summer sunshine. The high jump was next, bringing Kat another personal best.

The shot put and the 200 metres followed and Kat gave strong performances. The first day had gone by like a dream. Kat loved competing in front of this enthusiastic crowd. Even the presence of cameras and journalists couldn't put her off her stride.

Day two began with the long jump and Kat's biggest achievement so far. She jumped an epic 6.31 metres. It was a third personal best, and her biggest improvement yet!

Next was the javelin – another solid effort – and then the final event, the 800 metres.

Kat was top of the leader board. If she could beat the Latvian athlete Laura Ikauniece, her nearest challenger, in this last race, the gold medal was hers.

Mike Holmes was waiting on the touchline. The Harriers head coach had recently taken over her training. 'This is a good event for you, Kat,' he said. 'You're tired, I can see it. But you've still got it in you, if you want it enough.'

Kat's legs felt like lead. Her whole body ached. But she knew that the moment she stood on the start line, it would be a different matter. 'I can do this,' she replied, smiling.

As the starting gun fired, Kat felt a familiar energy surging through her body. Adrenaline. Her brain urged her long legs forward, and her legs obeyed, powering up to a stride. Running 800 metres would take her twice around the track. She must not lose sight of Laura.

Halfway round. *Keep ahead,* she told herself. *Keep ahead!*

One lap. *Keep up the pace!*

Two hundred metres to go. All the girls would have kept something back – that final bit of strength to allow them to sprint for the finish. Kat knew every single one of them would give it their all. She mustn't let anyone past. Especially Laura. *Pick up the pace! Go for it! Sprint! Sprint!*

The muscles in Kat's legs were screaming. Laura was beside her. She could feel her pumping arms and legs, churning the air. She was dimly aware of the shouts of the crowd. *Dig deep!* she thought. *Come on!*

Kat tumbled across the finish line and collapsed on to the track. She had kept Laura behind her. She had done it. She had won.

As she lay looking up at the bright blue sky, she realised: she, Katarina Johnson-Thompson from Liverpool, was World Youth Champion!

The other girls buzzed around her, offering hugs

and congratulations. Laura Ikauniece, who had won silver, and Kira Biesenbach, from Germany, the bronze medallist, set off around the track for a victory lap. But Kat was too exhausted to move. When she finally summoned the energy to use her aching legs, she had the track to herself. Someone handed her a Union Jack and she jogged slowly around the stadium, holding the flag high, smiling, as the crowd cheered her on. This was her moment. Every one of her hopes and dreams had been focused on winning an international competition.

It felt right. Shy, modest Kat was where she wanted to be.

Once the victory lap was over, Kat returned to the touchline, where Mike and her two biggest fans, her mum and grandmother, were waiting. They had been watching every step, leap and throw of the competition.

Her mum pulled her into a hug. 'I'm so proud of you, my love,' she whispered. 'You deserve this.'

Mike was grinning ear to ear. 'Great performance,

Katarina – 5,750 is a terrific score. And five personal bests! That long jump would have been enough to win an individual gold. You did yourself proud.'

But Kat's smile was wavering. 'I could have done better,' she said quietly. In her mind were the seven personal bests that she had wanted to achieve. It was always the throws – the shot put and javelin – that let her down and lowered her score.

Mike nodded. One of the things he liked most about Kat was her drive. She never stopped pushing herself. 'There's plenty of time, Kat,' he smiled. 'Don't let anything take away from what you've done today.'

And she didn't. Up on the podium, receiving her gold medal, Kat cried tears of pride and happiness. As the National Anthem rang out across the stadium, and the Union Jack was raised up the flagpole, it felt like a dream, completely surreal. *I made this happen,* she thought to herself. *This is the best day of my life. This is what I want to do. This is who I want to be.*

CHAPTER 8

A FAIRY GODMOTHER

The London 2012 Olympics were still three years away, but all eyes were already on the competition – including Kat's. Would she make the grade in time to compete alongside the likes of Jessica Ennis at the Games?

Mike was cautious. Kat was World Youth Champion. He knew she was more talented than even Jessica Ennis had been at sixteen. Kat had achieved the highest score at Under-18 level in the whole of British heptathlon history, beating Jess's record. But he had seen plenty of talented youngsters reach their peak in their teens then drop away. Could Kat sustain her potential? Did she have what it took to compete at senior level?

Deep down, Mike felt sure Kat had much more to give. It was his job to make sure she kept on growing as an athlete, and he was formulating a plan. There would be plenty of hard work to come: strength training, weights, more focus on Kat's weaker events – those troublesome throws. But it was important that Kat didn't crumble under the pressure. She was still a teenager. She had only just finished doing her GCSEs! Kat loved sport with a passion and Mike wanted to keep it that way.

There was a problem though...

The Harriers training ground in Wavertree was becoming too small to nurture a promising young athlete like Kat. The equipment needed updating. Everything was crammed together. Mike watched as Kat practised her high jump – she could barely take three strides before she leapt. *She needs a proper run-up*, he thought. *She needs to go to Sheffield or Manchester for training.* The high jump facilities there were much bigger and better equipped. *And she needs a gym membership.*

Mike sighed. All these things would require money. Kat had a Lottery grant that covered some of her training costs, but neither the Harriers nor Kat and her mum would be able to afford the extra expense. London 2012 would only happen for her if they could find help somehow.

If only a fairy godmother would wave her magic wand.

* * *

'There's post for you, Kat,' called Tracey. 'I don't recognise the handwriting though.'

Behind Tracey, in the kitchen, Kat was wrestling with her sports bags, which were overflowing with kit. Travelling light was not an option for a heptathlete with seven events to prepare for. Lugging her equipment on the bus between home, school and Wavertree was one of the things she liked least about training.

'Handwritten?' Kat spun round. Who would be writing her a letter? 'Do I have time to read it? I can't miss the bus.' She glanced at the kitchen clock. Just enough time.

She tore open the envelope. The header read 'Barrie Wells Sports Foundation'.

'Oh!' she cried as she started to read. 'Oh. Wow!'

'Who's it from?' asked Tracey, glancing over her shoulder. 'What does it say?'

'It's from someone called Barrie Wells. He is looking for young athletes to fund ahead of the Olympics. He's offering to fund me: £8,000 a year for training and equipment and whatever else I need.'

Tracey's eyes grew wide: £8,000? That was a huge amount of money.

'He funded Jessica Ennis. He paid for her physiotherapy. He's funding Steph Twell, the 1,500-metres runner, and Hannah Miley, and lots of others. He supports 18 young athletes every year.'

It seemed almost too good to be true!

Kat continued reading. 'His grandfather was a pole-vaulter and world record-holder, called, er... Ernest Latimer Stones. He says he loves sport and has chosen this way of using his wealth to help people. Mum, this is amazing. I'll be able to travel to Sheffield for training. And Manchester. I'll be able to get new equipment—'

'You'll be able to get a taxi to Wavertree so you don't have to carry all those bags about,' added her mum. 'It sounds like a brilliant opportunity, Kat.'

Mike was also delighted when he heard the news. 'Congratulations, Kat! Barrie is from Liverpool, you know,' he added. 'He's a huge football fan.'

Kat grinned. 'He must be okay, then!'

So it was agreed. Kat accepted Barrie's funding and in return, she became an ambassador for his sports foundation, which also provided access to sports for seriously ill children across the country. Everyone around Kat breathed a sigh of relief. It hadn't been a fairy godmother Kat had needed – it had been a fairy godfather!

And there was more...

Barrie knew how much Kat loved Liverpool FC. She had told him about playing football in the street as a child, wearing her Number 8 shirt, while her mum wanted her to be doing ballet practice. Barrie had organised a special surprise for her. Together they travelled to Anfield, where her showed her to his executive box overlooking the halfway line.

'You're a VIP today, Kat,' he told her as they climbed the steps. 'There's someone I'd like you to meet.'

As he flung open the door, Kat's eyes fell on the smiling face of Steven Gerrard. Number 8. Her Anfield hero! Kat's expression flicked from shock to amazement to elation. She was in the same room as Steven Gerrard!

'Consider it a reward for your amazing World

Youth Championship performance,' Barrie told her.

'I can't believe it!' laughed Kat. 'This is even more exciting than a medal.'

CHAPTER 9

OUT OF ACTION

Just ten days after her Italian triumph, Kat was on a plane to Serbia to compete in the European Under-20s Championships. With two major championships in under two weeks, she had to learn techniques for recovery. Her body had never worked so hard.

She triumphed again. This time as she stepped onto the podium, Kat was crowned European Junior Champion. Her score was 400 points higher than Jessica Ennis's had been at sixteen. Mike felt more and more confident in the sparkling young heptathlete.

But, back in Liverpool, there was a niggle of worry in Kat's mind.

Her left knee was giving her pain every time she jumped. Her left leg was the one she used for take-off. Her whole body weight landed on that knee every time she leapt.

It's probably nothing, she thought. *It'll sort itself out.*

But as the weeks went on, the pain got worse. From a small twinge, it had become a sharp, shooting pang. Kat was beginning to dread her training sessions. She started taking painkillers before she jumped – but the pain refused to be ignored. Kat couldn't hide her discomfort any longer. She knew she had to tell Mike.

'Kat, you can't keep injuries to yourself!' her coach scolded her. 'You could do lasting damage by training when you're in pain.' He shook his head. Kat was so young. Her body was still developing. 'We need to get you to a specialist.'

Kat grimaced. Her worst fear was that the doctor

would tell her she couldn't jump any more. Her stomach churned with dread. But Mike was right. She couldn't bury her head in the sand. She must pray that her injury wasn't serious...

There was bad news. The doctor diagnosed patellar tendinopathy, also known as Jumper's Knee. 'It's caused by overuse of the patella tendon, just below your knee,' she explained. 'Jumping and landing strains the tendon. It gets gradually damaged. With all the training and competing you do, Katarina, your tendon doesn't have time to repair itself.'

'So what do I do now?' gulped Kat.

'You must rest,' said the doctor. 'No question about it.'

There was horror in Kat's eyes. 'For how long? Can I train?'

'It's going to take months to heal. No jumping. Nothing that puts strain on your knee. You've done serious damage here.'

Kat's eyes filled with tears. No training? No

competitions? While her competitors were working hard, pushing their points tallies upwards, she would be sitting around doing nothing, getting weaker. She could see London 2012 disappearing before her eyes.

The doctor saw her dismay. 'You'll recover, Katarina,' she said gently. 'You can still exercise, but you must be careful.'

Mike nodded. 'We'll make a plan, Kat. You won't be sitting around, don't worry.'

Kat found her injury hard to bear. Without the pressure of jumping every day, the pain in her knee was decreasing. But she missed the thrill of competition, and the weeks of focused training leading up to each one. She missed the camaraderie of her Harriers teammates. She missed the incredible sense of achievement every time she hit a new personal best. She still went to Wavertree, but she felt broken and second-best.

Tracey could see her daughter's unhappiness and did her best to distract her. As the months went by, there were her A-levels to focus on. Going out with her friends. Parties. Football matches. Cuddles with her beloved dachshund, Chorizo. But all Kat wanted was to be well again.

There was one thing that still made Kat smile though: the achievements of her friends. The year 2010 had marked a breakthrough in Jodie's acting career. She had performed professionally onstage for the first time and had been given parts in *Holby City* and *Waterloo Road*. It was completely surreal for Kat, watching her best friend on TV! And while Kat was sad at missing out on the whole of the 2010 athletics season, she was pleased and proud that Jodie was getting the success she deserved. She felt sure that, one day, everyone would know the name Jodie Comer!

* * *

Over a year had passed since Kat's return from injury, and now 2012 had arrived: the year every athlete had been waiting for. The Olympic Games were coming to London in August, and there was just one thing in Kat's thoughts as the training season began: achieving the 5,950 points she needed to qualify for the London 2012 Olympic squad.

Kat hoped to do that at the prestigious Multistars competition held in early May in Desenzano del Garda, Italy. She fondly remembered competing at the World Youth Championships in Bressanon a few years earlier. She loved Italy, with its majestic mountains – and delicious pasta and pizza!

At 19, Kat was the youngest athlete in the Multistars competition. But she and Mike had been working hard on technique, and she was determined to make her mark among the more experienced athletes.

First up was the hurdles. Kat won her heat easily, smashing her personal best. Her time was the second fastest overall. Boom! Second on the leader board!

In the high jump, she cleared 1.81 metres and

retained her position in second. Would her luck hold? The shot put was next, always her weakest event. Kat gritted her teeth, sent a smile towards Tracey who was watching from the stands, and flung herself into the throw. It was another personal best: 11.75 metres!

As if the day couldn't get any better, Kat achieved yet another personal best in the 200 metres, and moved from second place to first. First place on the leader board! Kat could hardly believe it!

She prayed that her good form would continue on the second day of events, and although she ultimately slipped from first position, let down by her performance in the javelin, she still finished in bronze medal position. Competing against a field of older, more experienced athletes, it was a huge achievement. What's more, she had broken Jessica Ennis's British junior record!

But the best thing of all: she had secured a mighty 6,007 points, enough to qualify for the Olympic squad.

Kat could hardly believe it. In just three months, she would be competing at London 2012. Her first Olympics! Between now and August, there would be plenty of hard work, Kat knew. Mike would push her harder than she had ever been pushed before. But right now, she couldn't keep the smile of excitement and pride from her face. The Olympics! It didn't get much bigger than that!

Thank you, Italy, thought Kat. *I love you!*

CHAPTER 10

LONDON CALLING

It was 27 July 2012. As twilight fell over London, a feeling of nervous anticipation swept across the city and the country. The eyes of the world were on the capital and the brand-new Olympic stadium in Stratford. Inside the arena, 80,000 spectators were in their seats, ready to watch the opening ceremony, with many hundreds of millions more watching glued to their TVs across the globe.

'Ladies and gentlemen, welcome to London and to the Games of the thirtieth Olympiad.'

The show that followed was an epic spectacle celebrating the UK, the Commonwealth and the city of London. The crowd watched, mesmerised, as centuries of British history were brought to life by actors, musicians and dancers. Even the Queen played a starring role, performing in a brief sketch with Daniel Craig's James Bond!

Eventually the floodlights went up. It was time for the athletes' parade. Kat watched in wonder as competitors from all 204 Olympic nations streamed into the stadium: athletes, swimmers, cyclists, archers, horse-riders, wrestlers, fencers, gymnasts, boxers... the number was mind-boggling.

This is happening, thought Kat. *This is really happening... and I'm part of it!*

As Team GB, led by the cyclist Chris Hoy, carrying the Union Jack, entered the arena, confetti rained down on them and the crowd went wild. Kat had never heard a sound like it. Her cheeks hurt from smiling, but she couldn't stop. She was brimming with pride to be part of this incredible global celebration of sport!

* * *

The week that followed felt like a month. Kat was longing to be back in the stadium! But finally the big day arrived. Day eight: the start of the athletics events.

Down on the track, Kat looked around her with wide eyes. The stands were bursting with spectators, their excitement brimming over in noisy cheers. Among them was her mum, Tracey, along with the rest of her family. As the TV camera rolled past, Kat smiled and waved, then caught sight of her face projected in epic scale on the big screen. Eek! That would take some getting used to!

On either side of Kat, the athletes sank to their starting blocks, ready for the 100-metres hurdles. An electric tension filled the air, finally cut through by the bang of the starting gun and the roar of the crowd. Kat darted from the blocks. From now on, every microsecond was a series of calculations.

The length of her stride. The angle of her body approaching the hurdle. The position of her feet as they took off and landed. She channelled every ounce of power, speed and precision into these movements.

Seconds later, Kat raced across the finish line, behind a handful of more experienced athletes. Was it fast? It had *felt* fast.

The results appeared almost immediately on the huge electronic screen. More cheers. Kat was fourth in her heat. With a time of 13.48 seconds, she had equalled her personal best!

Giving each other hugs and pats on the back, the athletes left the track. They were all aware that it was the next heat, heat five, that the spectators were *really* waiting for. This was the race Jess was running in: Jessica Ennis, the best heptathlete the country had ever known, Great Britain's gold medal hopeful. Kat held her breath. She felt almost as nervous as if she were running the race herself!

If the noise had been extraordinary before,

now it was out of this world. A shiver went down Kat's spine. The expectation of every single British supporter was on Jess's shoulders. But there was also support and adoration. Jess was a hero.

They were off!

Kat didn't take her eyes from the 26-year-old as she rocketed from hurdle to hurdle, crossing the line in first place with a huge grin on her face. The crowd had hoped for a sparkling performance – and Jess had delivered.

But how fast had it been?

Kat's eyes flew to the big screen. A world record! The crowd were on their feet, a sea of red, white and blue. Kat's heart thumped with pride. Jess deserved this moment and the stadium reverberated with sheer, unbridled joy.

One event down, six to go!

Next up was the high jump, Kat's best event. *The crowd will have calmed down by now*, she thought. *They'll be waiting for Jess again. They won't be interested in my jump.*

But she was wrong. Even before she began her run-up, the crowd were clapping her: a slow, steady handclap, like a chant, ringing through the stadium. They were with her – this huge stadium crowd was right behind her, willing her to succeed!

Kat's surprise turned to adrenaline. She felt it surge through her legs as she sauntered into her run-up. When she took her jump, it felt like flying.

There was a wild eruption of cheers as she soared over the crossbar – 1.89 metres. Kat's hands flew to her face. She couldn't believe it: a personal best in her first Olympic high jump, in front of a cheering home crowd.

A huge smile broke onto Kat's face. This was surreal. Utterly surreal. A moment she would cherish forever.

The shot put and 200 metres followed, and day one of the heptathlon was finally over. Kat was in fourteenth place on the leader board. Jess was leading, in gold medal position.

The sun had set over London by the time Kat

arrived back in the Olympic Village. Once again a grin broke over her face. This small pocket of east London was home, for one extraordinary month, to over 10,000 athletes from 204 countries. How amazing it felt to be part of this huge international community! Athletes were strolling in and out of the accommodation blocks, laughing and talking, exploring their new home. A hubbub was coming from the vast dining hall where hundreds – no, thousands – of athletes were sitting at the long tables, eating, laughing and talking. The whole village was buzzing with fun and laughter and camaraderie.

How different it will be, thought Kat, *when the competition begins again tomorrow!*

CHAPTER 11

SUPER SATURDAY

The next day, Saturday, dawned bright. Kat felt refreshed as she strode into the stadium for her fourth event, the long jump. She gave another strong performance and the crowd cheered their enthusiastic support.

But, once again, it was Jess who led the field. Her performances had been flawless. Every time she entered the arena, she was greeted with cheers of wild delight. By the end of the day, with just one event to go – the 800 metres – the gold medal was firmly in her grasp. Jess had only to finish the race and she would be crowned Olympic champion.

The hopes of a nation rode on her shoulders!

First, though, it was Kat's turn to race. She was 16th on the leader board. As she took her place on the start line for her heat, she beamed for the TV cameras. She had loved every single magical moment of these two days, and the audience could see it shining in her face.

As the starting gun fired, Kat was quickly overtaken by the more experienced competitors. The pace was fast, but Kat was keeping up. She remained close at the back of the leading group as they completed the first lap. But Kat knew she had more to give. With 50 metres to go, she began to propel herself forward. Urging her tired legs faster, she overtook first one, then two, then three runners. Her heart was thumping as she powered across the line in second place. She had given her all.

With a time of 2 minutes and 10.76 seconds, she had smashed her personal best!

But before Kat could find out her overall ranking, there was the final. All eyes, including Kat's, were on Jessica Ennis. Kat watched as Jess pulled sharply away, leading the field for the first 500 metres. But with 300 metres to go, three runners edged past her, led by the world champion, Tatyana Chernova.

Kat's heart was in her mouth. *Come on, Jess! Come on!* She had seen her teammate fight back many times before. So had the crowd. Their confidence in her was total. *Come on, Jess!*

They were rewarded.

Approaching the final 100 metres, Jess rocketed forward. When she finally crossed the line, it was with a clear lead, her arms held victoriously in the air. Not only was she the winner but she had also set an incredible new world record!

Kat whooped for joy. It was exactly the finish that she, the crowd, and the nation, had hoped for. Great Britain's first athletics gold of the Olympics! Her heart went out to her brilliant, talented, hard-working teammate. Watching Jess was an inspiration. Would she, Kat, one day taste the glory that Jess was enjoying?

As she ran back onto the track to embrace the heptathlon queen, Kat knew she would do everything in her power to deserve future Olympic glory as much as Jess did right now!

* * *

Kat's final score was 6,267 points, placing her fifteenth out of thirty heptathletes overall. Friends, family, coaches, commentators... everyone agreed that it was a brilliant achievement for such a young athlete. At just 19, Kat had been the youngest in the squad. Destined for greatness? The next Jessica Ennis? A lot of people seemed to think so!

Back in Liverpool, Tracey, Jodie and her rest of her friends celebrated Kat's Olympic achievement with as much energy as Kat had put into her 800 metres. Kat glowed with pride. It was almost like she'd won a medal herself!

The Olympics marked the end of the season. Finally, it was time to relax. Kat's next stop that summer was the Bahamas. Throughout her childhood, she and Tracey had made regular trips to visit Ricky, but as a teenager, with the pressure of training, Kat hadn't seen so much of her dad.

Ricky was bubbling with joy to see his Olympian daughter and, it turned out, so was the rest of the country. The Bahamas had their own national team, of course, but they were also on Team Katarina.

'Watch this, Kat,' said Ricky. 'I recorded it for you. I think you'll like it.'

He flicked on the TV. On the screen, Kat saw herself in the Olympic stadium, preparing for her day-one high jump. As the crowd in London clapped along, the Bahamian commentator introduced her with as much pride and excitement as if she'd been a homegrown athlete:

'Our girl, Katarina Johnson-Thompson...'

'Dad, that's amazing!' Katarina felt like crying. It gave her a warm glow inside to think that here, over four thousand miles away, she had as much support as she had back in Liverpool.

'You're one of us,' Ricky said, smiling. 'Never forget, you belong here too.'

And the sunny Bahamas really did feel like home to Kat. Everywhere they went, she was welcomed like one of the family. It was clear to Kat that Ricky talked about her to his friends and neighbours all the time!

'You'll have to stop it, Dad,' she joked. 'People will be so disappointed when they meet me and find out how normal I am.'

'Impossible!' Ricky pulled her into a hug. 'I'm so proud of you, my beautiful girl. Isn't it lucky your mother let you give up ballet lessons!'

They both dissolved into giggles. The days of dance classes, leotards and ballet shoes felt so long ago!

'Mum's become the biggest sports fan ever,' smiled Kat. 'She gets so nervous though. It almost makes me nervous.'

Ricky grinned. 'She's invested.'

'I wish she'd chill out a bit sometimes!' Kat laughed.

* * *

It was soon time for Kat to swap the beautiful beaches of Nassau for a busy training season. Her next international event would be in August 2013 – the 2013 IAAF World Championships heptathlon in Moscow. It was only her second ever senior championship. Her target? To finish in the top eight.

Kat had taken her A-levels the previous year and had begun a degree in Sports Science at Liverpool John Moores University. In a whirl of training, studying, and more training, August and the world championships came round very quickly.

All British hopes were riding on Kat this time. Jess – now Jess Ennis-Hill, following her wedding earlier in the year – was out of action with a muscle injury. Tracey watched from the stand, swallowing her nerves as Kat ran, jumped and threw. By the end of day two, the tension was nail-biting. With only the 800 metres to go, there were seven athletes with enough points to win bronze – Kat among them.

Cheered on by Tracey, Kat ran her fastest 800 metres ever. It was an epic performance, but not quite enough to take her into bronze medal position. She finished in fifth with 6,449, a personal best, 28 points behind the bronze medallist, Dafne Schippers from the Netherlands.

Kat was delighted with her performance. But a question was gnawing at her. Had her ambitions been too modest? She had easily made the top eight. Should she be aiming for international medals now? That bronze had been tantalisingly close...

She sighed. There was one big thing that was holding her back: those tricksy throws. In the shot put, she had finished a disappointing 31st out of 33 competitors. She would have to improve if she wanted to claim a medal next time.

* * *

Kat didn't have too long to wait till the next international competition. Apart from the annual world championships, the biggest event in the multi-event calendar was the Hypo-Meeting in Götzis, Austria in May. Past winners included a 'who's who' of Kat's greatest heroes, from Daley Thompson in the men's decathlon to Denise Lewis and Jessica Ennis in the heptathlon.

Jess wouldn't be competing in 2014. She was pregnant with her first child. So, once again, everyone was watching Kat.

Kat rose to the occasion and shone. She set a personal best in the javelin, won the long jump and stormed to victory in the 800 metres. Even Tracey's nervous text messages couldn't put her off! This time, she was a medallist. A gold medallist! Kat received her honour with a smile that lit up the stadium.

Next up, in July, would be the Commonwealth Games in Glasgow.

And this time, Kat was the favourite.

CHAPTER 12

PRESSURE

'Ta-da!' With a flourish, Tracey unfurled her masterpiece. 'What do you think, Kat?'

Kat let out a peal of surprised laughter. 'A banner! It's brilliant, Mum!'

Tracey smiled. 'Eye-catching, isn't it?'

Several metres in length, with huge letters spelling out Kat's double-barrelled name, the banner was going to be unmissable.

'Wow, my name really is a mouthful, isn't it? This is so thoughtful, Mum, thank you.'

'It's your first Commonwealth Games,' Tracey smiled. 'We had to do something special!'

Kat visualised herself in the arena, catching sight of the humongous banner. She grinned. 'I love it. And I'm glad you're all coming to watch.'

This time, the whole extended family would be there in the stadium. Tracey had hired a minibus to take everyone to Glasgow where they would stay for a week and soak up the atmosphere of the Games, as well as being there to cheer Kat on in her seven events.

'We wouldn't miss it for the world,' said Tracey. 'Your nan's so excited.'

* * *

With a little over a week to go before the Games, Kat's final training was going perfectly to plan. Kat was working hard and Mike was full of encouragement. He knew, now Kat had tasted gold at Götzis, that she was hungry to be on the podium again. Mike, like everyone else, was optimistic that this would be Kat's competition.

Just a few days before the event, Kat was at Wavertree as usual. Mike was surprised to hear Kat calling out to him from a bench at the side of the training hall.

'I–I can't feel my foot. I think it's cramp.'

Mike ran over. Kat's left foot, her take-off foot, was badly swollen. Her face was full of anxiety. 'I can't put weight on it. Look, I can't even get my trainer on.'

Mike frowned. So close to a major competition, an injury like this was very bad news. 'We won't do any more training today,' he said. 'Go home and let me know how it feels in the morning.'

He helped Kat to hobble outside and into a taxi. 'Hopefully it'll be back to normal in a few hours,' he told her.

Kat braved a smile. 'It's already feeling a bit better. Fingers crossed.'

The pain soon went away and Kat went to bed relieved. But the next morning, the discomfort returned. Kat rang Mike and they went straight to the physio, who recommended a scan.

Once the scan came back, the answer was clear.

'It's a stress-fracture,' the physio reported. 'Tiny – but that's where the pain is coming from. It'll only get worse if you jump on it before it's healed. You could do long-term damage.'

Kat looked at Mike. He shook his head. 'There isn't enough time. Not for the Commonwealths.'

Kat let out a sob of dismay. Her first Commonwealth Games. She wanted desperately to compete in front of a home crowd. How disappointed her family would be! And Tracey's banner – it would go to waste! Tears trickled down Kat's cheeks. 'I can't believe I'm going to miss out,' she whispered. 'It's not fair.'

'We'll focus on the Europeans,' said Mike. 'Hopefully you'll be fit again by then.'

But by the time the European Championships came around in August, Kat's fracture still wasn't fully healed. Seven events wouldn't be possible, not with an injury, but could she enter the individual long jump? She couldn't bear the thought of missing the competition entirely!

Mike remained cautious. 'It's too risky,' he told her. 'We need you fully fit before you compete in any event.'

***

Missing out on two major championships was the hardest challenge Kat had faced so far. Sitting on the sidelines was so tough. Every week when she wasn't competing felt like a year. She couldn't shake the fear that her body simply wasn't strong enough for the seven gruelling events of the heptathlon. Now when she trained, she thought less about pushing herself and more about not getting hurt. Her self-belief was crumbling.

All that kept her going was the thought of Liverpool FC and their extraordinary 2005 UEFA Champions League Final. If they could pull through so could she. With the support of Tracey and her friends, Kat gritted her teeth and did battle against self-doubt. She trained as much as she could. She took care not to push herself too hard. Slowly her strength and determination gradually came creeping back.

And whenever she needed cheering up, there was one thing guaranteed to make her smile.

CHAPTER 13

BRONX AND CHORIZO

'Oh, I hope they'll get on okay!'

Kat wore a nervous expression on her face. In her arms, she held a tiny brown sausage-shaped creature, squirming to be released.

'Chorizo,' she said, addressing the handsome dachshund who sat on the ground in front of her. 'This is Bronx. Be nice to him!'

Chorizo had been part of the family for several years. How was he going to react to a new arrival? Kat placed the puppy on to the floor. The two dogs took a cautious step towards one another, before the younger dog, Bronx, launched into a bouncing, whirling frenzy, tearing wildly round the older dog before rushing off to explore the room.

Kat turned to Tracey. 'Well, someone's happy!'

'He's adorable!' smiled Tracey.

Chorizo watched Bronx in confusion for a moment before following him, tail wagging, on a tour of the room.

'You realise he's going to chew *everything*, don't you?' Tracey warned. They were in the living room of Kat's new house. 'Nothing will be safe any more.'

Kat laughed. 'I don't mind! As long as he doesn't chew Chorizo's tennis ball. That will cause trouble.'

But, of course, the puppy made a beeline for Chorizo's beloved tennis ball as soon as he spotted it. Chorizo turned to stare at Kat with horror in his big brown eyes.

Kat stroked her dog's head. 'Don't worry, Chorizo, his mouth is too tiny. Look!' The tennis ball was bigger than Bronx's head. His whole body was barely bigger than a banana.

'Oh, he's the cutest thing.' Tracey bent down to

tickle Bronx as he scampered past. He responded by rolling on to his back, kicking his short legs frantically in the air. 'Will he calm down as he gets older, I wonder?'

'I hope not,' grinned Kat, and Tracey laughed. How good it was to see her daughter smiling again!

By the end of the day, the two dogs were happily curled up, side by side, in Chorizo's basket. Kat let out a sigh of relief. How awful it would be if the dogs hadn't become friends.

'I've taken a million pictures,' she said, waving her phone.

Chorizo already had his own Instagram account. Bronx would be a photogenic new addition. How cute they were together!

Tiny Bronx was fearless too. By the end of the week, he could wrestle a toy from Chorizo's mouth. Chorizo's dinner wasn't safe either.

'That dog needs some training,' said Tracey.

'Already sorted,' said Kat. Her packed schedule now included weekly puppy training classes. 'We start tomorrow!'

But excitable Bronx was slow to grasp the idea of training. Sit? Stay? There was just too much to explore! And once he was off, he was off...

'Bronx! Bronx! Come here!' called Kat. 'All the other puppies can do this now. Come back!' Finally Kat gave in and chased after her runaway sausage dog. 'Bronx – focus, please. You're letting us down.'

Kat's competitive spirit was kicking in. She was determined that Bronx would succeed.

'We're going to get it right,' she insisted, fondling his velvety ears. 'We're going to practise all this at home.'

By the end of the year, Bronx's training still had a way to go. But Kat herself was fully fit again, and ready to start competing. She was determined to make 2015 her best year yet.

And she began it in style...

In February, she jumped a spectacular 1.97 metres to break the British high jump record at the British Indoor Championships in Sheffield.

A week later, she set a new indoor long jump record at the Birmingham Indoor Grand Prix: a stunning 6.93 metres.

Then, in March, at the 2015 European Indoor Championships in Prague, she broke the British pentathlon record.

'See, Bronx – what you can achieve with a bit of focus,' she laughed.

Kat's eyes were on the World Championships in Beijing later in the year – and after that, the Rio Olympics in 2016. Her goal was to exceed two metres for the high jump and more than seven metres for the long jump. And, of course, there were her other five events to prepare for as well. Kat's training schedule looked like a school timetable, with sessions in every discipline, plus hill runs and weights training.

Even when she wasn't on the track or field at Wavertree or Manchester, Kat was thinking about her performance. As Beijing drew near, Mike encouraged her to visualise each event in turn, to picture what might go wrong and how she could overcome it. As she lay in bed, the whole heptathlon would play out in her mind. On a good day, she would see victory.

Her mantra? *Run faster, sprint harder, fly higher, do yourself justice!*

CHAPTER 14

GREAT EXPECTATIONS

From her viewing point, Kat gazed with wide eyes at the city of Beijing stretched out below. Weird and wonderfully shaped skyscrapers towered up towards the sky, while on the ground, tangles of glittering highway wound through the city. Dominating the view was the Chinese National Stadium, known as the Bird's Nest, its interior lit with fiery orange and gold.

Kat was in Beijing for the 2015 World Championships. It was only her second World Championships, following Moscow two years earlier. Back then she had set herself a modest target and exceeded it. With Jessica Ennis-Hill only just back in competition after giving birth to her little boy, Reggie, this time Kat was the favourite to win.

In just a few months, everything had changed for Kat. The interview requests had begun to arrive, from newspapers, magazines, blogs. She was quizzed about her training regime, what she ate, what she wore. She thought back to when she was 19 and people had started calling her the next Jessica Ennis. Then, it had felt like a joke. Now, it felt very real. She could feel the pressure weighing down on her, pressing in on either side.

Kat blinked. The expectations, the pressure, it all felt as surreal as the view. Thrilling but scary.

The big question... Was she ready?

* * *

A familiar feeling of nerves and elation swept over Kat as she stepped into the Bird's Nest stadium the next morning. The day started well. She finished a respectable third place in the hurdles – Jess's strongest event – but beat the Olympic champion in the 200 metres and high jump. She was 13th in the shot put – but she had become used to losing points in the throwing events and compensating for them with her strong running and jumping.

At the end of the first day, Kat was second on the leader board, behind Jess in first place.

Silver medal position. So far, so good!

The second day had two of Kat's strongest events: the long jump and the 800 metres. She knew she could beat Jess with ease when it came to jumping.

First up was the long jump. Kat trained her eyes on the sand pit. Each fibre of her body knew what to do. She flew along the run-up and propelled her weight onto her left leg. Then she was up, soaring over the pit. In her head, she told herself: *Don't land, don't land, don't land...*

Finally Kat tumbled down into the sand. She sprang straight back up, eager to know her distance. But, no one was clapping. No one was cheering.

There was silence and... a red flag!

Kat's heart sank. A red flag meant a foul. Her take-off foot must have overstepped the take-off line and hit the plasticine board behind it. The long jump rules were strict and the officials were watching the line on a screen.

She walked back to the other end of the run-up, gearing herself up for her second attempt. *Play it safe*, she told herself.

She sprinted and leapt into the jump, cautiously this time, mentally measuring the distance as she placed her foot for take-off.

But – another foul. Surely not! Kat shook her head in despair. She had one more chance left. In a split second she decided to go for it – to aim for a big jump and not hold back. She rocketed along the runway, legs and arms pumping, then – she was up! She kicked vigorously in mid-air, propelling herself forward before plunging back down to earth.

It was a huge jump! Getting up out of the sand, she clenched her hands into fists, beaming with delight. Finally! But – wait... the officials were crowding round the take-off board again. The red flag hadn't been raised – what was going on?

Anxiety flooded into Kat's head. She joined the group bending over the board. A jumper's foot was allowed to touch the plastic covering of the board, as long as it didn't make an indent in the plasticine underneath. Surely she had just grazed the plastic? There hadn't been any pressure?

'Check. Can you please check?' she pleaded.

While the officials removed the board from its position and examined it, Kat hurried to the sidelines where Mike was watching every move.

'You're doing the right thing,' he told her. 'If there is any doubt, always argue the case. Clearly there is doubt or they would simply have raised the flag.'

'I didn't feel my foot touch the board.' Kat's face was all confusion. 'I'm sure I didn't.'

The wait was unbearable. Had her left foot scuffed the plasticine? Had she made an imprint?

Finally an official raised the red flag. On to the screen flashed the dreaded decision: three Xs. Three fouls. Kat would get no points for the long jump.

It was over. There would be no medal for her in Beijing. Unless her competitors had similar bad luck, she would finish at the very bottom of the leader board.

Kat's shoulders slumped in dismay and her eyes welled with tears. Jess appeared next to her, having just completed her own jump. She put her arms round her teammate.

'I know how you're feeling,' she whispered. 'It's awful to lose out this way.'

There were still two events to go. Kat had to carry on. Despite knowing she would come bottom, or close to it, she wouldn't be allowed to pull out. Unless they were injured, all the heptathletes had to finish the competition.

With the javelin out of the way, it was time for the 800 metres, the final event. Kat and Mike had agreed a strategy: she would get through it with minimal effort. She would save her energy to compete in the individual long jump event a few days later. Perhaps she would be able to salvage some Beijing glory that way.

Now that she was at the bottom of the leader board, Kat's heat contained the weakest competitors. She could have beaten them easily if she was trying. But she wasn't. She let the other racers leave her far behind. At the end of the two laps, Kat trailed across the line in last position and barely out of breath. She felt sad and, worse, she felt ashamed. She had let everyone down. Herself, her mum, Mike, her fans.

At the side of the track, Phil Jones from BBC Sport was waiting to interview her. She walked slowly over to the camera and Phil held out the mic.

'That must have been tough,' he said.

Kat mustered a smile. 'It's been a disappointing day,' she said. And, blinking back tears, she described her frustration at the horrible long jump result.

'But I know we're going to see plenty more from you,' Phil said encouragingly.

As soon as the mic was switched off, Kat's tears began to fall. She didn't care that she was probably still being filmed. There were cameras everywhere at the World Championships. The tears kept coming and coming.

Shortly afterwards, Kat sat on the sidelines and watched Jess triumph in the 800 metres final to win the gold medal. One thing was for sure – as heartbroken as she was, Kat couldn't begrudge her teammate her victory. Jess had worked so hard to get fit again after having a baby. She was a worthy winner.

But while Jess savoured her victory, Kat's confidence was shattered. She had finished in twenty-eighth position. How was she ever going to come back from this?

CHAPTER 15

ROAD TO RIO

Kat was back in Liverpool. Surrounding her were her loving friends and family, plus the snuggly, adorable duo of Bronx and Chorizo. She was back in training, doing the events that she loved. But the joy had gone out of it. The smile had left her face.

'You have to learn to move on, Kat,' Mike told her. 'You have huge talent. A bad day is just a bad day. Nothing more.'

Kat gave a little smile. She knew all about bad days. So much could go wrong in the heptathlon.

'I'm trying,' she murmured.

But Mike had a nagging feeling that there was something more to Kat's gloom. 'It's the pressure, isn't it?'

Kat nodded. She wasn't used to the spotlight. She had always been in the background while Jess shouldered the public expectation. Before, she had been competing for herself. It was so different now that everyone expected amazing things of her. When she didn't succeed, there were journalists writing about it, online trolls telling her she was a failure.

'It's too much,' she said quietly. 'There are so many people saying things about me. I just want it to stop.'

Mike sighed. Everyone could see Kat's talent. But she was still so young, only 21. She hadn't yet developed fully as an athlete. If only people could understand that!

'You have plenty of time,' he said. 'Move on. Shut everything else out. You have to, Kat.'

But try as she might, Kat couldn't put Beijing out

of her mind. She had worked so hard – only for it all to come crumbling down! When she visualised the next championship, she could see only failure.

'We need to focus on Olympic qualification,' Mike reminded her. 'Décastar is the next challenge.'

The Décastar event in Talence, France, in September 2015, was Kat's next opportunity to secure the points she needed to qualify for the Rio Olympics. She summoned her strength and her positivity. She had bounced back before. She could do it again.

By the time she arrived in France, it seemed to be working. At the end of day one, she led the field. With the nerve-wracking hurdles and the dreaded shot put out of the way, she went into day two feeling confident. She added a strong 200 metres to her success. With just two more events to go, she was feeling good.

The javelin had never been Kat's strong point, but she had been receiving special coaching from Goldie Sayers, the leading British javelin thrower.

Kat had been visualising her throw for weeks before the competition: memorising every step of the run-up, the angle of her body and her arm as she flung the javelin and watched it arc through the air...

Now she just needed to make it a reality.

But as she launched into the run-up, her thigh muscle gave a sharp twinge. *Focus,* she told herself. *Ignore the pain. Throw.*

She flung her body into the throw, before crumpling with pain as the javelin left her hand. Her score: a disappointing 29.15 metres.

Kat limped to the sidelines and her physio rushed over.

'You've pulled your adductor,' he said.

Kat grimaced. The pain in her leg was agonising; she was lucky to have managed the throw at all.

'My knee is hurting too,' she said. 'The left one. Even more than usual.'

The physio frowned. He knew Kat's history, the patellar tendinopathy she had suffered a few years earlier. Kat had had regular knee issues ever since, and she often took painkillers before she jumped. 'You won't be able to run the 800 metres,' he said. 'No way.'

Kat put her head in her hands. Her mind flashed back to Beijing and that horrible long jump. Another competition over! Another failure! She couldn't believe it.

There was one silver lining though: even without the 800 metre race, she had secured enough points to qualify for Rio.

If I'm fit enough to compete, that is, she thought gloomily.

* * *

Kat's medical team sprang into action as soon as she was back in Liverpool. The adductor would heal itself with rest and care. Her left knee was a bigger problem though. Scans showed a bone growth in her knee that was pushing into her tendon. Kat needed an operation.

To an athlete, 'operation' is the most horrific word in the dictionary. Kat fought back a tidal wave of fears. Would it go well? Would she recover successfully? Would she still be competing at the same level afterwards?

Tracey tried to reassure her. 'Of course it'll go well, love,' she said. 'You'll be fit again in no time.'

But the kind words of friends and family couldn't soothe Kat's anxiety. 'I'm falling apart, Mum,' she cried. 'The heptathlon is breaking me. I'm not sure I'm strong enough for this.'

'Every athlete gets injured,' Tracey said. 'You're doing one of the toughest sports there is. Even as a dancer, I got injured. But I always came back. Always. And you will too.'

Kat summoned a smile. She knew she had inherited some of her mum's stubbornness. Setbacks were tough to deal with, but deep down she knew she would never give up.

'Thanks, Mum,' she said.

'I believe in you, sweetheart,' said Tracey, holding her close. 'I believe you're destined for great things. You've already achieved so much.'

Hobbling around on crutches after her operation, Kat's achievements felt very far away to her. But she thought about the 2005 UEFA Champions League Final between AC Milan and her beloved Liverpool. *Never rule out the underdog. She might be injured. She might be down. But she would come back fighting.*

So she channelled every bit of determination into her recovery, into getting back to Wavertree, getting fit, getting back into competition.

But something was missing. Everyone could see it. With a pang of sorrow, Tracey realised that her daughter didn't smile any more. She didn't smile on the track. She didn't smile in training.

Would Rio put the spring back into Kat's step? The smile back on her face? Her mum prayed every day that it would.

CHAPTER 16

HAVE
FAITH

In his apartment in Nassau, Ricky Thompson was glued to the TV and the coverage of the 2016 Rio Olympics. He had already watched his daughter compete in the 100 metres. Her time, 13.48 seconds, was 'disappointing', according to the commentators, but in Ricky's eyes, Katarina was already a winner. He didn't see his daughter often these days, but she was always in his heart and he was brimming with pride for her. His apartment was full of photos and newspaper and magazine cuttings, celebrating her success.

It was time for the high jump, Kat's best event.

Ricky leapt up from his chair, flung his front door open and called into the street. 'It's my daughter's high jump. Katarina is about to jump. Our girl, Katarina! Come and watch! Quickly!'

Everyone in Nassau knew Kat's name. Soon there was a large group of spectators – friends, neighbours and strangers alike – piled into Ricky's living room. On the TV, the stadium crowd hushed as Kat began her run-up. Ricky could barely contain his excitement. He whispered the little prayer that he always spoke before she competed. *God protect her. Make her strong.*

It was as if Kat had a jetpack on her shoulders as she sprinted down the runway. Ricky had never seen her run so fast. He could see the concentration on her face, the focus in her eyes. From her left leg, she launched into a turbo-powered jump, twisting in mid-air and flipping on to her back to curl gracefully over the crossbar. The bar was steady, showing no sign of toppling. It was 1.98 metres, a personal best!

The crowd in the arena cheered with appreciation. Ricky leapt to his feet, flinging his arms into the air. 'Katarina! My girl!' He whirled around the room, clapping his new friends on the back, shaking hands and giving hugs. 'That's my Katarina!' he cried. 'She's going to win gold! I tell you. She's going to win this.'

It was a stunning performance. But, 6,000 miles away, in the Maracanã stadium in Rio de Janeiro, Kat struggled to share her dad's delight. She knew by now that a great performance in one event wasn't nearly enough to win the heptathlon. Even with this huge jump behind her, anything could still go wrong.

The truth was, Kat didn't want to be here in Rio. The fear of another injury was constantly in her mind. Old injuries were causing her discomfort. Her self-belief was at rock bottom.

She longed to be back home in Liverpool, safely away from the spotlight, away from the pressure and expectation. When she tried to visualise standing on the Olympic podium, receiving a medal, she couldn't. If only she could flick a switch and turn off the endless stream of worry and doubt!

By the end of day one, Kat was too far down the leader board to be a medal contender. Once again, it was Jess who was excelling. She was in silver medal position, exceeding every expectation, while a young Belgian athlete, Nafissatou Thiam, was in gold medal position. Nafi was two years younger than Kat, new to international competition, and brimming with talent. Hope, ambition and excitement shone from her face.

I used to feel like that, thought Kat to herself. *Now I'm just disappointing everyone.*

Kat dreaded the start of day two. As she went from event to event, a day had never felt so long. Finally, it was time for the 800 metres, the last event. Night had fallen over Rio; the athletes would run in the bright glare of the floodlights. Usually Kat loved to run at night. The glow of the stadium lights was thrilling. But tonight she felt flat. Her legs felt heavy. She wished she were anywhere but here. Anywhere at all.

Only the thought of how much her family and friends, in Liverpool and Nassau, loved and supported her, gave her the boost she needed. The 800 metres was one of her strongest races. She would go out there and do her best.

The starting gun fired. The runners were away. As the group picked up speed, Kat propelled herself into fifth position. Jess was in the lead, with Nafissatou Thiam trailing at the back of the group. As they went into the second lap, Kat powered into fourth place. She dug deep, tried to find the energy to propel herself forward into third, but the two runners ahead of her still had more to give. They sped away, racing each other to the finish line, leaving Kat far behind.

In a matter of seconds, the points had been calculated to give the athlete's overall scores. Despite a disappointing performance in the 800 metres, the talented newcomer Nafi Thiam had taken the gold medal. Jess had won silver. Kat trailed behind in sixth place.

If this had been four years ago, back at London 2012, Kat would have been thrilled at coming sixth out of thirty. But right here, right now, with world championship glory behind her, it was a huge blow. As the finalists, led by Nafi, circled the track together for their victory lap, Kat's face couldn't hide her misery.

Jess jogged over to her and they ran side by side. 'Kat, are you okay?' she asked.

'It's hopeless,' Kat whispered. 'I've let everyone down. I don't think I want to do this any more.'

Jess's eyes filled with pity. 'I've been there,' she said. 'We've all had highs and lows. When you're down, you need to keep believing that the next success is just around the corner.'

It felt to Kat as though there had been nothing but lows, setback after setback. 'All I'm doing is failing, Jess. What if I'm just not good enough?'

'You are,' Jess insisted. 'You're so talented,

Kat. You have to have faith that it'll all come together eventually.'

Jess knew there wasn't much she could say to comfort her teammate. She could see Kat's confidence was shattered once again. If only Kat could see that setbacks were there to make her stronger.

'I believe in you, Kat. You need to believe in yourself.'

CHAPTER 17

BROKEN

Mike was worried. Back in training in Liverpool, Kat was suffering injury after injury. He could see anxiety written all over her face. Her confidence had never been so low.

Something had to be done. Something had to change, and he made up his mind to speak to her.

'I've been thinking, Kat. High jump has always been your biggest strength, hasn't it? If you had been competing in the individual high jump in Rio, rather than heptathlon, your jump would have won you the gold. I think you should focus on that from now on. Become a high jumper.'

Kat blinked. She stared at him blankly. 'And give up the heptathlon?'

Mike nodded. 'One event rather than seven will put much less strain on your body. You won't get injured as much. You'll be able to relax a little.'

Kat's face broke into a frown. 'But I love the heptathlon.'

'You *used* to love it,' Mike said, shaking his head. 'I don't think you've loved it for over a year.'

Kat couldn't disagree with this. On the track in Rio, she had wanted to give up. But hearing the idea from someone else, a spark of stubbornness flared up inside her. 'I want to keep going, Mike. I still have more to offer. I'm sure of it. I don't want to give up.'

'It wouldn't be giving up, Kat. It would be refocusing your energy. Please think about it.'

Kat nodded. She knew as well as Mike did that things couldn't go on as they were. But she also knew that giving up the heptathlon wasn't the answer. There had to be another way.

And she was determined to find it.

* * *

By September, Kat had come up with an answer.

It was a risk.

It was scary.

It meant leaving behind everything she knew, everything that was familiar.

She needed a new coach.

Kat was so grateful for everything Mike had done for her. He had taught her all she knew. But it was time to move on, to push herself in different ways.

Mike understood. 'I'll always be wishing the best for you, Kat. You deserve huge success.'

Kat smiled and gave him a hug. 'Thank you so much. I hope my next coach is as brilliant as you are.'

But who would that next coach be?

Kat felt a mix of excitement and nerves as she began her search. Luckily, she had some expert help, from none other than former heptathlete and Olympic medallist Denise Lewis. If anyone could help her find the perfect coach, it was Denise.

'You may have to travel to find the right person, Kat,' warned Denise. 'First I want to take you to Amsterdam to meet Charles van Commenee. He was my coach while I was competing.'

Kat nodded. 'Yes, please.'

So together they travelled to the Netherlands and watched Charles as he led a training session with his team. Kat admired how driven he was. He and Denise had had a great relationship.

'I don't think he's the right coach for me though,' she admitted.

'We've only just started,' smiled Denise. 'There are a lot of people still to meet. I have a list!'

So, slowly but surely, they worked their way through the list, meeting coaches all over Europe. How interesting it was to see other coaches in action, to observe their techniques. She tried to imagine herself being trained by each of them. Would they push her? Would they support her? Would she have fun?

There were so many different styles, techniques and personalities. If only she wasn't so indecisive!

'Next we're going to Montpellier to see Jean-Yves Cochand,' Denise announced. Jean-Yves was a former athlete, who had been coaching athletics since Denise was a junior.

Kat recognised his name instantly. 'He's a legend!'

'Jean-Yves will be retiring soon,' Denise told her, 'but I'd like him to see you perform. His advice will be worthwhile, I promise you.'

'I hope so,' sighed Kat. They had met so many coaches and she was longing to find the right person and get to work.

* * *

'Katarina, you will never win a medal if you throw like that!'

Kat grimaced. Oh dear! Jean-Yves was one of the best coaches in the world. If he said her shot put was bad, it was bad. She hardly dared pick up the javelin now; she was scared of his brutal honesty!

'All wrong,' was Jean-Yves' verdict as she hurled the javelin into the throwing circle. 'Wrong – but you can fix it. Oh, yes, you can definitely fix it, if you work hard.'

Phew! That was all Kat needed to hear. She needed to know she was capable of improving, and Jean-Yves let her know that.

'I'll give it everything!' she said.

Jean-Yves nodded. 'I can see that. Stay here in Montpellier a few days, Katarina. That way we'll see if we can work together.'

Kat looked across at Denise and a smile spread across her face. For the first time in months, she felt hopeful and happy. She felt sure that Jean-Yves would be able to help her. His confidence and his honesty had inspired her. Denise grinned back. They were both thinking the same thing: *this could be it!*

Kat's stay in Montpellier was a success. She

enjoyed being out on the track with Jean-Yves and his colleague, Bertrand Valcin, who would be her main coach if she decided to stay. She ran and threw and jumped and was warmly welcomed by the French athletes who were also coached by Bertrand: Olympic decathlon medallist Kevin Mayer and European heptathlon champion Antoinette Nana Djimou.

With the bright Mediterranean skies above her, Kat was beginning to enjoy herself again. And for once, she didn't struggle with indecision. Her mind was made up. 'I want to train here in Montpellier!'

CHAPTER 18

FRENCH ADVENTURE

It was tough to say goodbye to friends and family and move to a different country, but Kat felt sure she was doing the right thing. Tracey was sad to see her daughter leave Liverpool. However, she could see the sparkle returning to Kat's eyes.

'It's going to be an adventure,' she told her. 'I'll support you whatever you do.'

'I'll call you lots,' Kat promised. 'And I'll be back in Liverpool plenty.'

Tracey wasn't the only one who would miss Kat. Bronx and Chorizo stared up at her with sad puppy-dog eyes as she prepared to leave. Why were there so many suitcases? Where was she going? When would she be back?

'Oh, Bronx, Chorizo, don't make this difficult!' Kat cried. She knew how much she was going to miss them. 'I'll be back to cuddle you soon, I promise. In the meantime, be good for your grandmother!'

***

Kat soon fell in love with elegant Montpellier. She enjoyed getting lost in the maze of narrow streets, filled with interesting shops and delicious-looking bakeries. There was the magnificent Arc de Triomphe, the bustling Place de la Comédie, and the towering St Peter's Cathedral, all made of the same warm golden stone. And beyond the city was the glittering Mediterranean Sea. Nassau, Liverpool, Montpellier... Kat realised that she had always ended up living by the water!

After a few weeks, Kat's training regime began

to take shape. She woke early most days, with the sun streaming through the window – Montpellier, she discovered, was one of the sunniest cities in France. She ate a croissant and a fruit shake before cycling to the training ground. There, she warmed up in the gym before heading out to the track with Bertrand. They would focus on one or two events in the morning, working with Kat's training partners, Kevin and Antoinette.

After a hard morning's training, she would tone her body with a sauna and an ice bath. In the heat of Montpellier, Kat was coming to enjoy the freezing ice bath!

In the afternoon she would go to the park to read, sitting on her favourite bench and enjoying the warm sunshine. It felt almost like being on holiday!

Life was good and Kat could feel her confidence returning. With Jean-Yves and Bertrand's expert coaching, she was getting stronger in every event. And it would soon be time to put herself to the test again...

In February 2017, Kat travelled back to Sheffield for the British Athletics Indoor Team Trials. She was back on form. She jumped 6.69 metres in the long jump and, best of all, the smile was back on her face.

Watching from the sidelines, Bertrand was smiling too. It was great to see Kat enjoying herself. He knew that if she continued having fun, her scores would go up and up and up. There was no limit to what she could achieve.

'Well done,' he told her. 'I think you're all set for the World Championships in London.'

A flicker of anxiety passed across Kat's face as her mind recalled the disastrous competition in Beijing two years earlier.

Bertrand read her mind. 'That was then, this is now. Everything has changed.'

One thing hadn't changed though. Jess had retired from international competition, and fans and commentators were still be making the comparison between them:

'The new Jessica Ennis-Hill.'

'The heir.'

'Jess's successor.'

Could Kat live up to Jess's huge legacy? She felt an enormous weight of expectation on her shoulders.

'You are no longer in Jess's shadow, Kat,' Bertrand told her. 'Your scores are already better than Jess's. Now, you need to prove that you can perform in the spotlight.'

* * *

While Kat had always thought of wise, supportive Jess as a mentor and not a rival, now she had a true rival: Nafissatou Thiam, the Olympic champion. Nafi was two years younger than Kat. Where Kat was weakest, the Belgian athlete was strongest. Her throws were enormous: she excelled at both shot put and javelin. Kat was stronger in the sprint and 800 metres, but Nafi was rapidly catching up with her scores in the high jump and long jump.

Kat knew she would need all her strength and skill to beat this formidable opponent. Nafi was focused, she was consistent, and she seemed to be unshakeable under pressure. And Nafi would be hungry to win the World Championship in London to add to her Olympic victory.

The battle was on.

CHAPTER 19

LOSS AND RIVALRY

Run faster, sprint harder, fly higher, do yourself justice...

Kat's favourite mantra ran through her head as she walked out into the London Olympic stadium for the 2017 World Championships. This place had such happy memories! Her mind flew back to the 2012 Olympics. She had been just a teenager then. No pressure, only the joy of competing for a passionate home crowd. How different it was now.

But Kat felt ready. She felt strong after months of training in Montpellier. She knew she must shut the pressure out of her mind, and focus on her performance.

Kat didn't expect to win the hurdles. There were stronger hurdlers in the field. She just needed a good score – and blazing over the hurdles behind the faster runners, she got it. She finished sixth overall, almost equalling her personal best. *So far, so good!*

The high jump was next. As usual, Kat expected to pick up extra points in her strongest discipline. The height was set at 1.86 metres. Fixing her eyes on the bar, she was away, bounding along the run-up, springing higher with each step. But her jump was too short. The bar toppled.

No matter, thought Kat. She would get over it on her second attempt. Away she ran – but once again, her leap sent the crossbar falling to the ground.

Everything was riding on her final jump. *Fly higher, do yourself justice.*

She ran. She leapt. She felt the impact as her back hit the bar. Not again! The bar fell away as she tumbled to the landing mat. No! Another failed jump!

Kat remained on her knees on the mat, her head in her hands. She had run out of chances. When she finally got to her feet, the crowd gave her a warm cheer of support. But without a strong score in the high jump, Kat knew how hard it would be to claw her way to a medal. Not against competitors like these. Not against Nafi Thiam.

In the evening, under the floodlights, Kat won the 200 metres with ease. But back at her hotel that night, it was the high jump she was thinking of. She wept tears of shame and disappointment. She felt like she had let her fans down. Worst of all, she felt like she had let her mum down. She wanted so badly to make Tracey proud!

Day two dawned clear and sunny. Kat shone in the long jump, but lost points in the javelin. Once again, she would be going into the 800 metres race with little hope of a medal. The home crowd cheered her as she crossed the line second – but she knew her points were not enough.

Nafi Thiam finished the race last... but with

6,784 points, she still won the gold medal easily.

Kat finished fifth overall, with 6,558 points. Another world championships. Another disappointment.

I'm still not tough enough mentally, she thought to herself. *I'm still letting myself get thrown off course by one bad event. How can I learn to stay strong when things go wrong?*

* * *

Coming back from a bad jump was one thing. But in November, Kat got a call that would change everything.

Seven thousand miles away from Montpellier, in Nassau, her father, Ricky, had died.

The shock left Kat reeling. He was just 59. As she travelled to the Bahamas with Tracey to say a final goodbye, sadness and regret filled her mind.

She knew how proud her dad was of her. He had loved to see her compete.

Grieving for her kind, loving father, with his big

laugh and even bigger smile, was the hardest thing Kat had ever had to do.

* * *

Losing Ricky was a wake-up call for Kat. As she travelled back to France to resume her training, there was just one thing on her mind. Her dad would never see her compete again, but she would succeed for her mum. She would prove her critics wrong. She would push herself to victory, whatever it took. She was determined that her mum would see her win.

She could do it.

She *would* do it.

Out on the track, Bertrand could see the new determination on Kat's face. Inside her, a new self-confidence was building. Whenever she felt doubt creeping in, she thought of Ricky. She was learning resilience. From now on, she wouldn't let anything hold her back.

She was ready to bring her A-game.

* * *

Kat's next competition was the World Indoor Championships in Birmingham in March 2018. She always enjoyed the indoor events. After all, there was no javelin, and that suited her just fine!

Do yourself justice. Kat was determined that she would. After a hard-fought competition, Kat won gold, a much-needed confidence boost.

Next, Kat's sights were set on the Commonwealth Games on Australia's Gold Coast. Once again, she rocketed to victory. Another gold!

But Kat returned to Montpellier in pain. She had injured her calf at the competition. It was a huge blow – a whole month away from training!

In the past, this kind of setback would have left Kat struggling with self-doubt. But the new Kat was determined not to be downhearted. This time, she only looked forward.

Do yourself justice.

Next came the European Championships in Berlin. Kat had missed lots of training because of her injury, but – *Bring it on*, she thought. *Bring on Berlin*. Nafi would be there and she was eager to test herself against the formidable Belgian. She was ready to push herself to her limit.

Kat finished in second place, behind Nafi who took the gold medal. But Kat was happy. She had not let her injury bring her down. She had stayed strong. She had kept motivated. Every fibre of her body ached, but it felt amazing to be standing on the podium, receiving her silver medal, knowing that she had given it her all.

And there was more. Despite her injury, Kat had earned a personal best score of 6,759. She was now in the world all-time Top 25 heptathletes, alongside Nafi, Jess, Denise, and the highest-scoring heptathlete in history, the American Jackie Joyner-Kersee!

Kat had proved her abilities. She had earned her

place in the heptathlon hall of fame.

There was just one question remaining. Would she – *could* she – beat Nafi Thiam?

Bertrand certainly thought so. And so did one other important member of Team KJT: Daley Thompson. Daley was a former Olympic gold medallist and decathlon world champion. Kat valued his encouragement and straight-talking advice. How lucky she was to have so many amazing athletes who supported and believed in her: Daley, Denise, Jess...

'She's so strong. So consistent,' said Kat. 'She seems unbeatable.'

'No one is unbeatable,' said Daley. 'Anyone is beatable. Even me,' he joked.

Anyone is beatable. That sounded like a great new mantra. Kat turned it over in her head. *Anyone is beatable*.

'You need to see rivalry as positive, Kat. That's how you push you yourself. That's how you grow.'

If anyone knew the benefits of rivalry it was

Daley. His long rivalry with Jürgen Hingsen, the German decathlete, was legendary.

'You're second in the world now,' Daley continued. 'Use that. When you're number two, you try harder. You're hungrier to win.'

'Thanks, Daley.' Kat smiled. His advice had given her a way forward. Embrace rivalry!

'Doha is coming up. You are good enough to be world champion. Make it happen, Kat.'

The World Championships in Doha, Qatar, were just a few months away. Everything Kat did was build-up for that competition. Every step. Every jump. Every throw.

Kat nodded. Could this be her year? She had failed on the world championship stage so many times now. After all her disappointments, she wanted a medal so badly!

Anyone is beatable.

Kat smiled. She knew Nafi's weaknesses.

And more importantly, she knew her own strengths.

CHAPTER 20

DOHA DREAMS

Kat sat in the call room inside Doha's Khalifa International Stadium, Qatar. Along with 30 other heptathletes, she was waiting to be called to the track for the start of the 2019 World Championships.

She was surrounded by familiar faces. Most of these women had been competing against her for years now. It was almost like a family, thought Kat. Unlike the sprinters, who often tried to intimidate each other before races, to psyche each other out, the heptathletes always had friendly words for one another. They respected each other. The heptathlon was simply too gruelling for mind games!

Kat glanced at Nafi. While groups of other athletes chatted, the Belgian athlete was sitting on her own, as she usually did before events. Nafi was always friendly, always polite, but she liked to remain inside her own quiet bubble before competing.

It certainly seems to work, thought Kat.

Because of the sweltering daytime temperatures in Qatar – up to 40 degrees even in September – most events were being held in the evenings and late into the night. Many athletes and coaches grumbled. But not Kat. She was a night owl. She found early-morning starts much harder!

When the athletes were finally called into the stadium, Kat had a broad smile on her face. The pressure was definitely on. Along with Dina Asher-Smith in the 100 metres and Laura Muir in the 1,500 metres, Kat was one of the favourites for a British medal. But she was learning to take pressure in her stride. After so many years feeling dread every time she stepped into an arena, now she felt bubbling excitement once again, just like she had as a teenager.

* * *

Up in the stands, Kat's most loyal and passionate supporter was ready and waiting. Tracey had watched all of Kat's competitions over the years. She had sat in hundreds of arenas and had seen Kat's confidence grow and crash again and again over the years. It filled her with joy to see her daughter happy and enjoying sport again. She prayed that Kat's hard work and determination would pay off this time.

Suddenly a ripple of applause started up. There they were! Tracey's heart gave a lurch as she spotted her daughter down on the track. The feeling of pride at seeing Kat in an international championship had never lessened. And the feeling of anxiety didn't either! Already her fingers were gripping the seat in front of her. *Relax!* she told herself. *They're not even on the blocks yet!*

Down by the start line, Kat was limbering up for the hurdles. Her scores were getting stronger in this race, whereas it was one of Nafi's weaker events. A win should be hers. Should be. Kat knew to take nothing for granted.

She planted her feet in the blocks and steadied her nerves. *Go!*

Kat was off, eating up the ground with every pace, striding gracefully over the hurdles. She overtook the leader, Annie Kunz, as they reached halfway, then she sprinted to the finish, well clear of the rest of the runners. Her time: 13.09 seconds. A personal best!

Kat's hands flew to her face and she let out a laugh of surprise and delight. Up in the stands, Tracey gave a whoop of joy. It was the perfect start!

But how would Kat fare in the high jump? It was here that her medal chances had unexpectedly crumbled at the World Championships in London two years ago.

Kat cleared the lower heights easily. The bar was

now set at 1.95 metres. She bounded along the run-up then leapt. For an instant, she seemed to hover in the air above the pole, before curling gracefully over the top and falling back on to the mat below. *Phew! Clear!*

Nafi Thiam cleared the same height, gaining the same points. But Kat was still in the lead thanks to her spectacular hurdles performance.

In the shot put, Nafi performed brilliantly as usual. An epic throw of 15.22 metres put her first in the event, and first on the overall leader board, overtaking Kat.

Kat knew she couldn't match Nafi's throw, but she needed to score well.

Her first and second throws were unimpressive: 12.33 and 12.38 metres respectively. She had just one attempt left. Kat visualised the throw, then used her force to hurl the shot strongly away. It landed with a thud at 13.86 metres: another personal best! Kat could barely believe it. She stared at the replay on the stadium screen. It was true! The throw of her lifetime! She spun around to beam at Bertrand, bouncing up and down with delight.

A personal best in the shot put? Who knew!

Nafi was still in the lead, thanks to her huge throw. But Kat was now only 51 points behind. Winning her 200-metres heat easily, Kat was soon back on top, leading Nafi by 96 points.

Day one was over.

It was late into the night as the athletes finally left the arena to return to their hotels. The beautiful curved stadium was lit up in glowing rainbow colours, while the sports complex around it dazzled with lights, like a fairy grotto. Beyond the city on one side was the Persian Gulf, on the other, the desert.

Kat was tired. She was hungry. But above all she was excited.

I *can win this,* she thought. *I can actually win this!*

CHAPTER 21

GOLD GLORY

When Kat woke the next morning, there were still hours to wait before the start of the competition. All the action would begin at dusk when the searing desert heat had lessened. There was something magical about performing at night, like being in a dream, Kat thought.

When day two's events finally began, it was with the long jump. It was her moment to put the pain of Beijing behind her. It was her moment to shine.

Kat flew down the runway, arms pumping. Springing from the take-off board, she hurled herself over the sand. She could barely bring herself to look up and check the colour of the flag. *Please don't be red!*

But the white flag was waving. The jump was clean – and long: 6.77 metres.

Phew! Kat now led Nafi by 216 points.

But the javelin was next. Nafi would score big, she knew.

Kat was first to throw, and she gave herself another cause to smile. Yet another personal best: 43.93 metres! On the sidelines, Bertrand flung his fist in the air in celebration. Nafi, who had an injury to her elbow, still beat her, but her throw was well short of a personal best. Kat would be difficult to beat now.

Sitting in the stands, Tracey dared to imagine a gold medal around Kat's neck.

Down on the track, as she prepared for the 800 metres, Kat did too. *Run faster. Sprint harder. Do yourself justice.*

But before they could run the final race of the

World Championships, there was the stadium light show. Since all the events in Doha were taking place at night, the organisers made full use of the dramatic night-time setting. Before each event, the arena plunged into darkness. Music played and coloured lights danced across the stadium while the competitors were introduced. As Kat was announced by loudspeaker, her name was projected onto the track in huge capital letters, while glowing ribbons of red, white and blue light rippled around the arena.

Finally the booming soundtrack ended and the floodlights came to life again, returning the arena to brightness. It was time.

The starting gun fired. Verena Preiner from Austria set a fast pace out of the blocks. Kat joined her at the front, along with the two American runners, Kendell Williams and Erica Bougard. The group of four pulled steadily away from the rest, with Kat running in third, behind Verena and Kendell. She was calculating her strategy with every stride. She needed to get ahead of them, but not too soon. It was always easier to have someone else to set the pace. But if she left it too long to overtake, Verena or Kendell might pull away – or Erica might steal her position in third. She would have to make her move soon...

Okay, now!

Kat summoned an extra burst of energy. Quick as a flash, she darted into the narrow space between the two leading runners, overtaking first Kendell, then Verena. As the bell rang to signal halfway, she was already pulling away from them. Would they fall back? Would they keep up with her? Would one of them find a final spurt of energy and challenge her for the lead? All she knew was that she had to keep the pace up. Being out in front made her vulnerable, blind to the action behind her. She couldn't – *wouldn't* – let anyone overtake!

With 250 metres to go, Kat accelerated again. Her long legs carried her flying down the home strait. She sensed she was increasing her lead over the others. She urged her tired legs onwards, faster, faster.

Come on! Come on! Over the line!

Kat jogged to a halt, stopped to catch her breath, then flung herself onto the track. She had done it! She lay there panting for several moments. Behind her, the other runners were tumbling across the line and falling to their knees, sprawling across the lanes. With seven gruelling events completed, every single one of them was exhausted!

Gold!

Kat had given it her all. She had won and – wait! Another personal best: 2 minutes 7.26 seconds! What a way to end the competition!

It had been an extraordinary two nights. A gold medal. Four personal bests. A victory over Nafi Thiam at last!

And with 6,981 points in total, she had also overtaken Jessica Ennis-Hill as the highest-scoring British heptathlete of all time.

When tears came to Kat's eyes, they were of joy.

Up in the stands, Tracey also had tears in her eyes. Her humble, hard-working daughter was world champion. *World champion!* Tracey had believed in Kat every step of the way, from the moment she exchanged ballet shoes for running shoes. She could not have been prouder of her amazing daughter!

On the sidelines, jubilant texts and tweets were piling into Kat's phone. From Jodie, Daley, Denise, Jess, Barrie Wells... everyone who had been on this incredible journey with her wanted to share this special moment. Kat was itching to read their messages of love and support.

But before she could do that, there was the small matter of the medal ceremony.

Kat had collected many medals over the years. She had stood on many podiums. But her first world championship medal was truly special. The proudest moment of her life so far.

And Doha did things a little differently with its ceremony.

Instead of a podium on the field, with the crowd

looking down on the athletes, Kat and her fellow medalists stood on a huge illuminated plinth, at the very top of the arena. Behind them were giant screens, each with an animated national flag, and huge CGI medals – a gold disc for Kat, a silver for Nafi and a bronze for Verena Preiner. There were real medals too, of course. Kat beamed with delight as her gold medal was placed around her neck. As the National Anthem began to play, more happy tears flowed down her cheeks. It was the moment she had been dreaming of – world championship glory at last.

This is for you, Mum, thought Kat.

CHAPTER 22

BRINGING IT HOME

Doha had put on a dazzling light show, but Liverpool was not to be outdone. To celebrate Kat's victory, the monuments of her hometown were lit up in red, white and blue. A giant gold medal hung from the town hall balcony, along with a huge banner: *Congratulations Katarina Johnson-Thompson.* Kat was the first person from the city ever to win a world championship medal – it was time to celebrate!

And, following her victory in Doha, it was becoming impossible for Kat to walk around Liverpool without being recognised.

'Katarina!'

'KJT!'

'Congratulations, Kat!'

'Our girl!'

Kat had never signed so many autographs or posed for so many selfies.

And the people of Liverpool weren't the only ones eager to welcome their homecoming champion.

'Bronx! Chorizo! Have you missed me?' called Kat as she stepped over the threshold of her mum's house, now home to her two beloved dachshunds.

The sound of eight small paws scampering wildly through the house told her that they had! The two dogs tumbled excitedly into her arms, nuzzling her, licking her, barking with delight. Kat adored sun-drenched Montpellier, but it would never have what Liverpool did: snuggles with her favourite furry duo.

'It's so good to see you, boys!'

Of course, Bronx and Chorizo had no idea of her achievements halfway across the world in Doha. And it seemed, they were the only inhabitants of

Liverpool who weren't interested in her medal.

'Look, Bronx! Look what Mummy won!' Kat took the precious gold medal from its box and dangled it in front of him. Bronx gave a suspicious sniff then pattered away.

'How about you, Chorizo? Don't you want to know what Mummy gets up to when she's not here cuddling you?'

No, Chorizo didn't. The shiny thing wasn't edible, and it wasn't a tennis ball.

Kat grinned at Tracey. 'They don't want me to get big-headed, do they!'

Tracey laughed. 'Your nan will want to show it to the neighbours, as usual.'

Kat giggled. Her nan had always showed off her medals, ever since her very first youth championships. Her family was so proud and it meant the world to her.

Kat fondled her dogs. 'Deep down I know you care too, boys,' she joked.

* * *

And there was more exciting news to come. In November, Kat was shortlisted for the BBC Sports Personality of the Year. The show would be broadcast live from Aberdeen on 15th December. The news was announced on social media by the Liverpool FC players Trent Alexander-Arnold and Alex Oxlade-Chamberlain.

'Sports personality of the year?' gasped Kat. 'But—' She could hardly believe it. She had watched the show since she was a child. Past nominees and winners included so many of her sporting heroes. 'Am I a sporting hero? Really?'

It didn't seem possible!

Kat's fellow nominees were Ben Stokes, Dina Asher-Smith, Raheem Sterling, Lewis Hamilton and Alun Wyn Jones. What an honour it was to be named alongside these incredible sportspeople.

On the morning of the show, Kat travelled back from Martinique where she had been training.

Her first stop was Aberdeen Children's Hospital. The children, who had spent months in the hospital, had written to Kat, asking if she would visit them.

Yes, of course she would! And she wanted it to be a surprise.

'Girls, boys, we have a visitor,' announced the chief nurse. 'Can you guess who it is?'

Walking into the surgical ward, Kat's heart leapt as she saw the stunned faces of her young fans. There were squeals and whoops and cheers. *Katarina! Katarina! KJT!*

'That was an amazing welcome, thank you, everyone!' smiled Kat.

The children had been joined by their parents and carers. Kat talked to everyone, signed autographs and posed for more selfies. Then she spotted a table football set. 'Who likes football?' she asked.

A little boy, Morgan, piped up. 'Me, I do!'

'Me too,' said Kat. 'I challenge you to a game, Morgan. Do you want to be red or blue?'

Morgan picked red. 'Because Aberdeen play in red.'

Kat grinned. 'So do Liverpool. But I guess I'll have to be blue this time.'

They took up their positions. The other children watched as they swung their plastic players back and forth, sending the ball from one end of the tiny pitch to the other.

'Goal!' whooped Morgan as he shot the ball past Kat's goalie.

'Goal!' shouted Kat as she scored a few seconds later.

But Morgan had the upper hand. The children giggled at Kat's dismay as she let in goal after goal. 'This is harder than it looks,' she laughed. 'Morgan, you're a worthy winner!'

'I beat KJT!' he whooped. 'I actually beat KJT!'

It was time to say goodbye. Kat was due at the BBC studio. Filming would start in just a few hours.

'Good luck, Kat!' shouted the children, their families and their nurses. 'We hope you win.'

'Meeting you lot, I've won already!' Kat grinned.

* * *

Kat was bubbling with excitement that night. The Sports Personality of the Year was so much more than a competition. She loved hearing the inspiring stories of sportspeople and coaches, who were making a difference in so many amazing ways.

This year's award for Unsung Hero went to Keiren Thompson from Nottingham, who ran a project called Helping Kids Achieve. His work gave confidence and motivation to so many young people.

The lifetime achievement award went to Tanni Grey-Thompson, who had championed paralympic sport for 30 years.

It was incredible to be on a stage with these inspiring people!

Finally, it was time to announce the main award, Sports Personality of the Year. The iconic trophy was ridden into the studio on a quadricycle by former rugby player Gareth Thomas, along with cricketer Graham Swann, and former athlete Dame Kelly Holmes, another hero of Kat's.

Ben should win this, she thought. *I think Ben will win.*

She was right. The trophy was won by Ben Stokes. The cricketer had had an outstanding year, leading his team to victory after victory. Kat cheered louder than anyone as he collected the trophy. The second worthy winner of the day!

And Kat knew she was also a winner. Being here in Aberdeen for this wonderful celebration, well, it was the perfect end to a perfect year!

* * *

But what about the future?

Kat would be part of the British squad travelling to Tokyo for the Games. Her greatest rival remained the Olympic champion, Nafi Thiam. To beat Nafi at the Olympics, Kat knew she would have to do something that no other British heptathlete had ever done: score over 7,000 points. She would have to excel not just in the jumps, but in everything. Even the shot put!

Could Kat do it? Well, she had learned how to deal with pressure and overcome setbacks. She was faster and stronger than ever. Her coach believed in her. Her friends and family believed in her. Most importantly, she believed in herself. A medal, even a gold, was now within her grasp.

Bring it on, thought Kat. *Bring on Tokyo. I'm ready!*

World Championship Medals

🏆 Sopot 2014: Long jump, Silver

🏆 Birmingham 2018: Pentathlon, Gold

🏆 Doha 2019: Heptathlon, Gold

NAME:	Katarina Johnson-Thompson
DATE OF BIRTH:	**9 January 1993**
PLACE OF BIRTH:	**Liverpool, UK**
NATIONALITY:	**British**
SPORT:	**Athletics**
Height:	**183 cm**
Main events:	**Heptathlon**
Club:	**Liverpool Harriers**
Coach:	**Bertrand Valcin**

Olympic Medals

GOLD **0**   SILVER **0**   BRONZE **0**

World Championship Medals

GOLD **2**   SILVER **1**   BRONZE **0**